The Men Files

The Men Files

What men really think about life, love, dating and a whole lot more . . .

HUMFREY HUNTER

headline

First published in 2011
by HEADLINE PUBLISHING GROUP

1

Cataloguing in Publication Data is available from the British Library

ISBN 978 0 7553 6167 0

Typeset in Cochin by Avon DataSet Ltd,
Bidford-on-Avon, Warwickshire

Printed in the UK by CPI Mackays, Chatham, ME5 8TD

HEADLINE PUBLISHING GROUP
An Hachette UK Company
338 Euston Road
London NW1 3BH

www.headline.co.uk
www.hachette.co.uk

To Rachel and Sarah

Contents

Prologue

The Men Files is a no-holds-barred, brutally honest depiction of how single guys work, how they think, what they want and why they do what they do. Inspired by what one man – me – learned in the immediate aftermath of the end of a long relationship, it is, in short, the book single women have been waiting for: the one that will finally decode the myriad of confusing signals which men, simple creatures that we are, give out both knowingly and unknowingly.

The Men Files will reveal the truth about guys – that they are complicated and inconsistent *but* also not as mysterious as they seem. And by reading the inside story of single men's lives and minds, you will learn how to spot guys who are not interested in commitment, how to make a guy ask you out and why men sometimes don't make a move, even when they want to.

Shortly after the end of the second of two long-term relationships, I started working as a dating columnist. The column made me do what very few single men ever manage – analyse the way men like me behave. This book goes much further than I could in the column and will tell you everything you need to know about men, all seen through the eyes of one normal guy – me again. With that knowledge you'll be able to play the single game with confidence, stay in control and, most importantly, have fun along the way.

And let me make one thing clear: this book is not a step-by-step guide to how to bag the perfect man. There is no such thing as a foolproof, 100%-guaranteed method to getting the man you want, because no two people are the same. Instead, this book will give you a vast amount of information about men to add to what you have discovered yourself. Once you've combined the two, you can work out your own personal set of dating rules and requirements. After that, the choice of whether or not you decide to gamble on someone is yours. All I can do is make sure you are well prepared and well informed enough to understand the risks you take with the single men you meet and that you understand the importance of putting your *own* knowledge and experience to good use.

That, then, is the ultimate purpose of this book: to use my time as a single man – all two-and-a-half years of it – and all the stories I heard from guys and girls along the way, to understand how and why men find and fall for the right girl at the right time.

First, let's go back to the beginning of those two-and-a-half years.

The Men Files open

As break-ups go, mine wasn't particularly dramatic. After three fairly happy years with my ex, I'd realised she wasn't the one I wanted to spend the rest of my life with, and the relationship ended.

So far, so normal.

But the next day, my friend Giles ordered me *not* to get a girlfriend for the next year. I was thirty years old and had been single for a grand total of six months in the previous eight years (during the gap between two long relationships). So Giles said I needed to 'meet' plenty of new girls before getting involved with another one.

According to Giles, this one-year rule was essential because I am soft and fall in love too easily. He said if I wasn't careful I'd end up with a new girlfriend long before I was ready for one, thus laying the foundations of yet another painful break-up a couple of years later.

During those twelve months I would be allowed to date as many girls as I wanted but any kind of commitment was out of the question. This approach was new to me – I'd never consciously *decided* to stay single before. But the more I thought about Giles's idea, the wiser it sounded.

After all, I'd had two long-term relationships and neither had worked out. My twenties were behind me and virtually all my friends were hooked up. Weddings and babies were cropping up and popping out all over the place and I was lagging behind in the quest for a grown-up life.

While my instincts might have told me to move faster and try to catch up by grabbing a wife and starting to breed as soon as I could, I decided Giles was right. I should take my time, learn about myself and the kind of girl I was compatible with, and only then, when I was ready and the girl was right, should I make my move.

Immediately, dating felt very different. I started analysing the women I met and my reactions to them in a new way and in more detail than ever before. My love life started feeling like a research project. It was fascinating.

Then, in a truly outrageous stroke of luck, I went pro-fessional. That is to say, I was asked to write a newspaper dating column. The guy who wrote it before me had just given up because he had got engaged (either a shame or lovely news, depending on how you looked at it), and they wanted me to replace him.

Suddenly my 'research project' was taken on to a whole new level. I was now a professional dater and had the perfect excuse to do as much as I wanted. After all, I wasn't just playing around for the sake of it – now everything I did was for the sake of my readers. They wanted to know how the mind of the single guy works and it was my responsibility to show them.

This also gave me the perfect opportunity to poke my nose into other people's romantic business, and I began to interrogate friends, both male and female, about their love lives. I heard stories about dates of all shapes and sizes. Some made me laugh and some made me blush while others simply left me speechless.

After nearly two years of reporting on my own adventures on the romantic front line, collecting experiences from countless other people and analysing them all, my research was very nearly complete. And the result was the idea for this book.

In it I wanted to help girls get inside the mind of a single man, to understand all the mistakes we make and why we make them, why we treat certain girls the way we do, how men behave through the stages of their own single phases and the signals we respond to positively versus the ones that make us run away scared. And so this book is about what happened around me and what happened to me; the stories I heard and witnessed; the advice I gave, took and ignored; and the wisdom and battle scars I picked up en route – with absolutely nothing held back.

Those stories will give you knowledge that, like a poker player thinking about percentages and odds, you'll be able to use when making your own dating decisions to maximise your chances of getting the result (or guy) you want.

Just as importantly, as well as revealing the secrets of how a single man's mind works, this book will prove that no matter how badly you think you've messed up in your love life, no matter how deeply you humiliated yourself with that guy you really liked, either I or someone I know has done far, far worse, because every story I tell is true. They didn't all happen to me (I would have lived a very strange life if they did) but they all happened to someone. And while this book is not, I'm happy to say, simply an account of my own romantic ups and downs and ins and outs (sorry – I couldn't resist that), when it's useful I will switch to confession mode and tell you stories from my own life.

And here's the best bit – once you single girls have read all the stories and realised that you're not actually the worst, most incompetent dater in the world after all, and that men are nowhere near as mystifying as they once seemed, your confidence will rocket . . . and everyone knows how attractive confidence is.

Before you start the first chapter, there is one other thing to mention. When I wrote my last dating column, my research for this book wasn't quite finished because I was still single. But I'm not single any more, because not long afterwards a girl arrived in my life completely unexpectedly, at a moment when I wasn't even looking for a girlfriend. In fact I'd just about given up on the idea. But this girl arrived anyway – and stayed. Her name is

Charlotte and you will see her name a fair few times on these pages. She also has her say at the end of the book.

And meeting Charlotte, I now understand, was the final part of my research, the final lesson I learned: the one that made me finally understand how, why and when a guy – me – meets someone special.

Chapter One

Meeting Men

- What men do to meet girls
- How men think when they approach girls
- Why the man who seems the smoothest isn't the safest
- How to spot a serial seducer

When a man meets a girl for the first time, very often there will be two questions going through his mind. The first is, 'Will she have sex with me?' and the second is 'How soon?'

I'm not going to explain, excuse or justify it. That's just the way we are.

OK, that's a worst-case scenario – I was deliberately lowering your expectations. We're not actually that bad, I promise. Some of us are, granted, but nowhere near all of us. But knowing where the worst of us are coming from is a useful starting point.

The fact is, there are guys out there who will say anything to get you into bed and I'm willing to bet that just about every girl in the world who's single for any length of time will find herself falling for these moves at least once.

Those girls have nothing to be ashamed of. Nothing at all.

All they've done is taken a risk and not got the outcome they wanted. There's no point dwelling on something that's been and gone, so if it's happened to you, move on. Don't worry about things you can't control, like the past. Just put it in a box marked 'EXPERIENCE' and do your best to ensure it doesn't happen again. Not because you've done anything wrong but because you felt bad afterwards. I want you to avoid feeling bad.

Now let me tell you how.

The rule

There is one simple rule you can follow that will statistically improve your chances of protecting yourself no end. I can't guarantee success every time but in the long run, the benefits will be obvious.

This rule can be dressed up in a hundred thousand different flashy ways (hell, people have even written books about it), but I'm going to put it as simply as possible.

It goes like this: if you like a guy, don't jump into bed with him too quickly.

Sounds simple, doesn't it? Yet a remarkable number of girls ignore the fact – and it is a *fact* – that the sooner you sleep with a guy, the greater the chance that nothing significant will follow.

Of course, if all you want from him is sex then jump into bed with him as soon as possible. I don't think it's wrong for girls to enjoy casual sex, by the way. But I do think it's easier for guys to have emotion-free sex than it is for girls, so the risks (the main one being falling for the person you're having supposedly casual sex with) are greater for the female half of the arrangement. That's not me being sexist or anti-feminist (I'm neither), it's simply a generalised conclusion based on a lot of observation. If you disagree, fine. But I'm not changing my mind.

As with all my stories and conclusions, there are exceptions to this rule. But like post-relationship-flings turning into marriage, there aren't many.

Why?

Twenty-first-century men are still men

Imagine a man goes moose hunting. He spends weeks, maybe months, planning his trip. He and his friends get all their kit together, clothes, guns, food, etc. They arrange somewhere to stay, decide who's driving and work out how much the whole trip will cost them. Hours and hours are sacrificed and the group are indescribably excited before they've even left home.

Eventually the hunting begins. They find a moose and oh, he's a magnificent creature. Tall and strong, with a noble head and spectacular antlers. Yes, he's the one they want, the moose of a lifetime. So they track him through the forest, moving as quietly as possible in order to stop the great beast from running away. For hours they follow, until one of the hunters sees his opportunity. He gets out his rifle in silence, loads it more carefully than he ever has before, breathes deeply and slowly takes aim. He knows this is the biggest and best moose he's ever seen, the greatest prize of his hunting life. He's worked so hard, put so much effort in for this moment. He's nervous and excited and he feels great.

And so the moose is killed (humanely, of course) and the men carry it back to their hotel, putting in some back-breaking work along the way. In the weeks that follow, the man who shot the moose has its head mounted so that he will be able to look on that noble face and those magnificent antlers forever, and tell any visitors to his house about the time he went out and hunted it. That moose's head means a great deal to him. He *values* it.

Now imagine exactly the same man is driving through a forest one day. An equally majestic moose is crossing the road as he's driving along and in an unfortunate accident his car hits the animal, which is killed immediately. The man gets out of his car and looks at the creature. He is a hunter and knows moose, so recognises this as a superior specimen. But what does he do? Does he take it home and mount the head so he can admire it for the rest of his days?

No. He shakes his head, thinks, 'That's a shame, poor fellow,' drags the dead moose to the side of the road and goes home. Presented to him under different circumstances, exactly the same moose was almost worthless.

That is how men think, particularly about sex.

Question: which moose do you want to be?

Answer: don't be a roadkill moose.

MEN SECRETS

Guys want to see you as a prize of great value. We want to feel like we're something special because we've got you. Understand that and you can use it to your advantage.

Signals and signposts

So how should you go about giving off the right level of flirtation, i.e. tell a guy you're fun but not in the buy-me-a-drink-and-I'm-yours-for-the-night way?

Simple: keep control. Decide what you're going to do and stick to it. Make rules for yourself. I don't mean following *The Rules* (I'll come to those later), I mean a set of guidelines devised by you and for you that will ensure you don't mess up.

How not to do it

A girl I know told me this story about a friend of hers. That source is genuine – this isn't one of those tales that begins 'You won't believe what my friend did . . .' but which really happened to the teller. Nor is it one of those Chinese whisper legends that spreads from one group of friends to another, each jump adding another layer of juicy embellishments.

No, this one really happened. I even know the name of the girl involved. But I won't put it in here because I'm not that mean.

So, the story.

Girl goes out on a first date with a guy she likes a lot. Girl has a history of going too far on a first date, especially when she's had a few drinks, and so resolves not to drink too much in order to keep herself under control. Girl even adds another layer of security by not shaving her legs or doing anything to her bikini line which, she believes, will stop her wanting to take her clothes off in his presence later that night.

But girl gets drunk and frisky, brings man home and comes

up with a cunning plan. Girl sits him on her sofa while she nips to the bathroom and does some quick shaving. Girl, by now hair-free and wearing a short skirt, slinks back to him and arranges herself seductively in the doorway of her living room.

Man looks her up and down and his eyes widen in horror when his gaze reaches her legs. Girl is confused and looks down.

Turns out that girl isn't very good at the gentle art of shaving when she's had a few too many cocktails and she's given herself a few nicks. Now her legs are covered in blood.

Girl screams.

Girl runs back to bathroom, locks the door and starts crying. Man knocks on the door and tells her it's not a big deal but she won't listen. She tells him to leave and they never see each other again.

Not much of a love story, really.

So what can she do? Either torture herself about the embarrassment for the next twenty years or laugh and move on, on the grounds that there's no point worrying about things you can't change. Besides, I'd bet my left leg she won't be making that mistake again.

As you can probably guess, I'd advise her to go for the latter option. But with one extra shot at glory: she should also have called the guy involved. If he was a good guy and liked her, the blood incident wouldn't matter. And if things worked out, they'd have something to laugh about for years.

Even if he wasn't interested she could hardly embarrass herself any more than she already had.

Lessons learned

How should she have played it? There is one simple thing she could have done that would have avoided all the hassle and humiliation: not taken the guy home in the first place.

There's nothing inherently wrong with sleeping with a guy on a first date but jumping into bed with a guy too quickly can cause problems if your goal is to maximise your chances of things going somewhere.

This girl made the wrong decision. She lost control of the situation and so lost the guy.

But it didn't have to be like that because in reality, all wasn't lost even after she'd kicked him out. If she'd called him the next day, said sorry and asked if she could buy him a drink some time, he might well have said yes, OK, let's meet up. She'd have got herself a second chance by taking control again.

Here I go again on my own

For any single guy, let alone one who is relatively new to it, approaching girls when you're sober is one of life's great challenges. What do you say? And how do you exit with any dignity if she blows you out? Both times I became single after a few years out of the game, after Girlfriend X and Girlfriend Y, I didn't have a clue.

But what I did have was a secret weapon: B.

B is a guy who will crop up regularly through this book. He's a good friend of mine but a bad, bad influence. The type who goes out drinking a lot and has a huge arsenal of chat-up lines that he uses on girls wherever he is, no matter what time of day or night it is. As a result, B dates several different women each week and when he's slept with a girl once, he loses interest immediately and moves on. He's a stereotypical player, a bad boy to his bones who has no interest whatsoever in settling down.

He is most definitely not a truly bad *person* – he's my friend and has kindly offered up his experiences and thoughts for this book in the hope they'll be useful – but B is fundamentally not someone I'd want one of my sisters to date. So he is exactly the kind of guy that you should know how to recognise, understand and avoid.

One more thing: if I do anything you don't like, it was B's fault, not mine.

Remember that, please.

Whatever it is, B made me do it.

B has a foolproof method for meeting girls. He's used it many, many times and swears it works. B's method is simple: you find a girl you like the look of, walk up to her, relaxed and smiling, look her in the eyes and say slowly, 'Excuse me, I hope you don't mind me saying, but you're absolutely gorgeous.' Pause for her to smile and blush a little then add, 'If you're not already attached, I'd love to take you out for a drink some time.'

In an ideal world, she says, 'Yes, that would be great,' and you exchange numbers and away you go. Apparently even when the girl has a boyfriend this move leaves her walking on air because a stranger thinks she's gorgeous, and you get a buzz from knowing you put that smile on her face. Everyone wins.

So I decided to try it.

In at the deep end

On the Tube early on a Thursday evening, I saw a gorgeous dark-haired girl. We were standing quite close to each other and when our eyes met and she smiled, I immediately started silently rehearsing B's line.

A few minutes later and after some more smiles she got off the train, two stops before mine. I quickly decided to go after her – this was too good an opportunity to miss.

Thankfully the platform was almost empty so if I was to be humiliated, there would be no witnesses.

I tapped her on the shoulder, she turned round and smiled. I took a deep breath and carefully recited the magic words. My speech went well. I was pleased.

Then she turned off her iPod, took out her headphones and I had to start all over again.

It was agony: the speech didn't sound anywhere near as smooth second time round because the pressure had cranked right up. As I finished, she gave me a beautiful smile (she really was gorgeous) and said, 'Sorry, I'm attached. But thank you.'

I said he was a lucky man (I couldn't think of anything else – B didn't prepare me for this eventuality) and off she went, leaving me crushed.

All over? Not quite.

When she got to the end of the platform (I had to wait for the next train – more agony), she turned round, waved and gave me a lovely, glowing smile. At that moment I realised that even if you make a mess of your words, like I did, a wholly unexpected move like that will at the very least brighten up someone's day.

But did I do it again?

No way – I have my pride to think of.

Chat-up lines and warning signs

This attempted seduction on the Underground was highly unusual for me. That kind of move has never been my style. The thing is, guys on the pull fall into one of two categories – the ones who fear rejection and the ones who don't. And I've always had the fear.

The ones who aren't bothered by being rejected won't wait for a bit of lingering eye contact and a coy smile from the girls they're interested in before they make a move. Instead, this kind of guy will march straight up as soon as he sees a potential 'hit'. If she turns him down, it's no problem. He'll simply go on to the next one to catch his eye without giving the first a second thought.

B does this. He'll spot a fit girl in a nightclub and say, 'Hi, I like your shoes – can I have your number?' and even if she gives him a stingingly contemptuous 'not in a million years' look and tells him to go jump off a cliff, he'll still walk away smiling and look for the next one. How he manages to do this night after night, I do not know. But he does. He even has a little motto: 'It's better to try and fail than to not try at all,' which he reminds himself of when his courage supplies run low. Which isn't very often because he is extremely successful.

The guys who actually fear rejection – a far, far larger group of which I'm a member – don't operate like this. We need encouragement from a girl, some signs that tell us we at least have a chance with her before we say hello. Maybe a smile and some lingering eye contact. Something that we can work through in our brains and end up thinking, 'I think I might just be in here.'

I don't class myself as particularly shy but compared to B, I sound like a wimp. I'm not, I promise.

MEN SECRETS
If a single guy sees a girl he likes the look of but doesn't approach her, he's scared of being rejected. That's the only possible explanation.

We're not shy, honest

I'll tell you two stories to prove this. The first, like the Tube story, happened to me during the six-month gap between Girlfriends X and Y. I was in a queue for a cashpoint near a club I was about to go into when I noticed a penny coin on the floor in front of me. I picked it up and looked around. Next in line behind me was a pretty brunette. I gave her the coin saying I needed the luck that act would bring, we started talking and I ended up dating her for a few weeks. Nice move, I thought. I was a little bit drunk at the time, which made things easier. But still, nice move.

The second happened to B. He was at the gym and, after fighting a losing battle with some weights, decided to get into the pool. B was paddling around in the pool getting a bit bored when a girl in a bikini came out of the changing rooms. She got in the pool, did a couple of lengths and then stopped right by where he was. As she got out, she smiled at him and he noticed she was very pretty and built like an extra from *Baywatch* (his words, not mine). B then had a great view of her from behind as she walked slowly into the steam room.

B waited a couple of minutes and followed her in. When he opened the door he couldn't see anything (it was a particularly steamy steam room) so he said, 'I know there's someone in here but I can't see you, so I'm sorry if I accidentally sit on your lap.' She laughed and they chatted for the next few minutes, until he started cooking in the heat.

Then they went for a post-gym coffee and she gave him her number.

Three days later, B was half an hour into his first date with the girl he met in the steam room. He'd found out she was funny, laughed a lot, and was one of those people who are fun to be around. So the signs were promising.

But there was trouble ahead.

She mentioned she lived near the gym where they met, so he asked her if she worked in the area.

'No,' she said. 'I'm just back for a week.'

'Oh. Back from where?'

'University.'

B nearly choked on his beer.

He had to ask the question, 'How old are you?'

'Twenty-one. How old are you?'

'Thirty.'

'Oh,' she replied, as if it didn't matter at all.

But B couldn't let it go because nine years is a long time. When he left school, she was seven. When he left university, she was still a couple of years away from choosing her GCSE options.

Suddenly the whole date felt wrong. B had absolutely no idea she was so young. He told me he'd have guessed early to mid-twenties, not because she looked older than she was but because she was so confident and self-assured it wouldn't have occurred to him that she was only twenty-one.

They had a few more drinks and he found himself enjoying the evening, even though he kept reminding himself how young she was. Eventually B decided to leave the age worries for another day and the date lasted until the next morning.

In the days that followed, B found himself in a bit of a quandary over this girl. He liked her and they had a good time but she was a twenty-one-year-old university student. Could that work?

Why men and women are different

A couple of nights later I was out for dinner with B and a few other friends, guys and girls around our age. He told them about this girl and the potential age issue because he genuinely didn't know what to do. The guys all laughed in a pervy, get-in-there-lad kind of way while the girls with boyfriends smiled quietly. But the single girls didn't smile. One of them really laid into him.

'You're pathetic,' she spat. 'You should be dating girls your own age. Guys who date girls that much younger than them are losers who can't handle mature women.'

I might not be the most mature person in the world but I thought that was harsh. So did B and he told her to stick her bitterness up her single backside. He was going to damned well carry on seeing the twenty-one-year-old if he wanted to.

But why had the single girl got so cross about it? Why had the idea of an older man with a younger girl aroused such a strong reaction?

Why it was sweet revenge

Every guy who has ever had a crush on a girl his own age knows what it feels like when you find out another guy who's interested in her is *older*.

A ball of helpless, self-pitying fear begins to form in your stomach as you realise you're competing for this wonderful creature against someone you cannot hope to match. Yes, you're fun, you worship her and you get on with her friends. You might even have a car and a decent job.

But he's *older*. And therefore inherently cooler than you.

That feeling is agony. It's frustrating and painful and makes us feel like pathetic little boys. Even if we meet the older guy and we're a foot taller than him and much better looking, it doesn't matter. He's *older* and so he wins and there's absolutely nothing we can do about it.

Probably the biggest heartbreak of my life happened to me in my early twenties in exactly that situation. My rival was eight years older than me and a whole lot richer and more worldly. Of course he didn't *get* her like I did. They didn't *connect* like we did. I knew that and I knew she knew it too. But that didn't matter. He was older and therefore I was out of the picture.

So when this girl started having a go at B for dating the

twenty-one-year-old when he was thirty, I could empathise with her anger because it was the same helpless rage we guys felt when girls our age swanned off with older guys, except she was sympathising with the 'innocent' younger woman who was being helplessly ensnared by the cunning older man.

But I also couldn't help but think this angry girl was the kind of female who back when we were twenty-two or twenty-three would have been all over a guy a few years older. She'd have thought it was cool to be with someone mature. She'd have given us guys her own age that patronising look and said something like, 'Older men are much better. They're *men*, you know? Not boys. You lot are boys.'

Unlucky, sweetheart. Things have changed now.

Of course I didn't say any of this – I'm not that brave. And I didn't want a drink thrown over me. B wasn't so shy and ended up wearing half a glass of Pinot Grigio for the rest of the evening.

B makes a decision

That evening out hadn't shed much light on B's dilemma about whether or not to carry on seeing the twenty-one-year-old. I saw him a few days later and he asked my opinion. I could tell he liked her so I gave him exactly the kind of advice I thought he would give me if I were in the same situation.

'I'll give you five reasons why you'd be stupid to walk away,' I said. '1) She's twenty-one and you like girls with hot bodies. 2) Your mates will all be jealous. 3) She's young so won't try to marry you straight away. 4) If you end it you're giving into peer pressure and that makes you a loser. 5) She's a student so won't expect you to spend lots of money on her. You're on to a winner.'

Those were the pros. For the cons, we went to a couple of female friends.

Firstly, they pointed out that steam room girl had student loans to worry about while B had a fairly grown-up job so what did they have in common? Nothing, they said. Secondly, they said her friends might be lovely but they too are twenty-one, which means they also have student loans to pay and lectures to attend while his friends were getting on in their jobs and thinking about marriage and children. How would the two groups mix? Like oil and water. Finally one of them referred to her jokingly as 'the child', which made B shudder slightly.

It took him until the next day to make a decision.

One of his friends rang him and when he answered her call, she said, 'Hello, is that B, the notorious paedophile?'

That was the moment when the chances of anything more happening between B and the twenty-one-year-old died. He might have given in to peer pressure in some people's eyes, but at least he wasn't the subject of public ridicule. And remember, this was only a fling. She was leaving town in a few weeks so probably wasn't looking for anything serious, and B is B so wedding bells weren't going to be ringing any time soon. But he still couldn't face the flak he'd get even if he only saw her for a few weeks. That's how important B's reputation is to him.

Personally, I thought he'd made a mistake. When he talked about this girl he didn't just come out with all the clichéd perviness you'd expect from a guy like B seeing a much younger girl. Obviously he did come out with some of that – B is what he is – but he also talked about how much he laughed with her and what a fun time they had had together. I hadn't heard him talk about a girl in that way for a long time so stopping seeing her was, in my eyes at least, a shame, because there seemed to be something potentially good between them. But it wasn't my decision.

MEN SECRETS

Guys worry about what their friends, both male and female, think of them and their choices. There are few things we want more than the approval of those closest to us.

I get something off my chest

You will have noticed from my previous couple of stories that guys go about pulling girls in different ways. Of course they do – no two people are the same, male or female. And different girls react in different ways to the same approaches.

Which is why books like *The Rules* and *The Game* annoy me so much.

Essentially, *The Game* tells guys to seem funny and interesting and then gives them lessons in how to win girls. However, as I see it, the book just helps guys to take advantage of girls who must have low self-esteem and/or are young enough not to have fallen for all that crap before. *The Rules* tells girls not to be too easy or too available, but in my view it just gives them lessons in how to get an insecure guy wrapped around their little finger.

And that's it.

Hardly rocket science.

Don't get me wrong, I'd love to sell a quarter of the number of books Neil Strauss and Ellen Fein and Sherrie Schneider have, but something about these approaches leaves me slightly cold.

My problem with both is that they make romance contrived and thus totally unromantic. My problem with *The Game* specifically is that I have sisters and lots of female friends and the idea that they could be manipulated so easily into going to bed with someone makes me feel a little bit ill.

Having said that, I read *The Game* and thought it was a brilliant book, utterly hilarious and a truly accomplished bit of writing. It was, though, the only book I have ever been embarrassed to be seen reading in public. Normally I have no shame. I've read Jilly Cooper on London's public transport system and being a 6' 4" man I looked slightly unusual, but that didn't bother me.

But the looks I got when sitting on the Underground reading *The Game* made me feel distinctly uncomfortable. 'Look at that guy,' people were thinking. 'He's either so much of a loser he needs a book to tell him how to pull or he's one of those guys who needs to sleep with every girl in the world to feed his own ego.'

Do you know why I thought that?

Because whenever I saw a guy reading *The Game*, that's what I thought about him.

So if you ever see a guy reading *The Game*, remember it's possible that he's reading it purely for entertainment.

That's why I read it.

Honest.

My *Rules* story

I was on a night out with my friend Charlie and his work colleagues when he pointed to a gorgeous girl, said she was single and offered to introduce me to her.

'Brilliant,' I said. 'Anything else I need to know?'

'She's blonde, funny, intelligent and has a great body. What more could you possibly need?'

'Great, let's go.'

Charlie stopped. 'Actually, there is something. She's a *Rules* girl.'

I considered this for about a nanosecond.

'Forget it,' I said. 'I'd rather date a blow-up doll.'

One last book rant

And then there's my all-time favourite relationship book, *Why Men Love Bitches*. Men love bitches? Really? I know lots and lots of men and I can't think of a single one who loves bitches.

I can't even think of one who *likes* bitches.

Actually, I'm being a bit misleading here. I know full well that *Why Men Love Bitches* doesn't really encourage women to be bitches. It just tells them to be true to themselves and not let anyone bully them out of that or- make them feel they're not good enough, which is a message I wholeheartedly agree with.

Just don't be a bitch about it.

Why guys go to pieces when they like someone

One of the most annoying things about being a guy is that it's very easy for us to date girls we like a bit but with whom we don't see any long-term potential. We are relaxed and cool with them. We don't get nervous and say stupid things that make them think we're weird, and we don't come on too strong and scare them away. We seem confident and sure of ourselves.

But put exactly the same guy in front of a girl he actually likes – one who makes him go a bit weak at the knees and who he can't stop thinking about – then it is perfectly possible, likely even, that he will go to pieces. He will be the opposite of the man described in the previous paragraph, despite being the same man.

You see, when a guy meets a girl with whom he can see potential, suddenly there is much more at stake than a few dates and some bedroom fun and games. When emotions rear their heads, men get confused and insecure. Spotting a confused man is, as I'm sure you all know, very easy. Finding one attractive is unfortunately much harder.

I suppose the point I'm trying to make is this: if you like a guy and at the start he seems a bit nervous and like he's trying too hard, don't run away. Wait for him to calm down a bit and let his confidence with you grow.

Remember: male confidence is a fragile thing.

What's in a name?

When I was younger it was my name that affected my confidence more than anything else. I didn't like it at all. No other kids were called Humfrey, everyone spelled it wrongly (an 'f' in the middle is way better than 'ph' – it's a fact) and I stood out wherever I went. It made me feel so self-conscious and awkward that I used to think about what I would change my name to once I was old enough. I seem to remember quite liking Steve as an alternative when I was about nine.

In many ways I was an odd child.

When I was old enough to start meeting girls, it became even worse. Now I had to talk to them and tell them my name, the potential for embarrassment was suddenly multiplied several thousand million billion times.

The worst moment came when I was at a party aged about nineteen and talking to two girls. That's right, two girls at once – I thought I was doing brilliantly.

Then I told them my name.

One of them said, 'No, really, what's your name?'

And that was it, game over. I blushed so hard I couldn't talk and had to spend the rest of the night sitting alone under a tree with a two-litre bottle of cider for company.

But as I grew up and became a bit more sure of myself, I began to like my name. And when I started to make my first forays into journalism and publishing, I realised how it was useful: there aren't many Humfrey Hunters around so standing out was easy. But I will never, ever forget how self-conscious I felt about it when I was younger.

Final thoughts

If a guy is *too* good at dating, by which I mean if he was clearly completely lacking in nerves when he approached you; if he took you somewhere unspeakably cool but behaved like he goes to those places every night of the week; if he knows exactly where he's taking you for late-night drinks before it's even suggested (he'll probably suggest something corny like 'a little place round the corner'); if when he kissed you at the end of the night there was no doubt in his eyes that you would kiss him back – that guy has dated so much that he could compete internationally. He might be good for a night out or two but the chances are you're just another girl sucked into his well-worn routine whom he'll get bored of pretty quickly.

I'm not saying be cynical about every guy you meet, just that if the guy you're dating is a little bit nervous, don't think badly of him for it. His uncertainty means either he likes you very much or doesn't date very often, both of which are good things from your perspective especially if, as often happens, they occur at the same time with the same guy. If he's completely cool and in control all night, if he's too smooth, then you're not special.

Remember again: male confidence is a fragile thing.

MEN SENSE:

1. The best guys aren't always the smoothest.
2. If a guy seems like he's trying too hard, it's because he likes you. So forgive him.
3. Read *The Game*, for two reasons: a) it's hilarious and b) to help you spot when someone is playing it on you.
4. Make up your own *Rules*.
5. Stick to those rules, even when you're drinking, because that will help you keep control.

Chapter Two

Inside the Mind of the Single Man

- How newly single men behave
- Why you should avoid them
- If you can't avoid them, how to cope with being someone's rebound fling

How it feels to be newly single

Between the ages of twenty-two and twenty-six I had a girlfriend for four-and-a-half years who will be referred to as Girlfriend X. She was followed six months later by Girlfriend Y, who I was with for three years from age twenty-seven to thirty. That means I was single for six months in eight years.

When I became single again, after three years off the scene with Girlfriend Y, it felt like I was driving back into a town I used to know like the back of my hand only to find a local council buffoon had installed an intricate new one-way system and a load of reorganised junctions which conspired to get me completely and utterly lost.

Which goes to show that when a man becomes single again after a long relationship, he is a mess. He might look OK from the outside – wearing clean clothes, exercising, eating plenty of fruit and vegetables and so on – and he might even sound OK.

But really he's not.

Inside he's nothing but a seething mass of contradictory and confusing impulses and urges, whether he was the dumper or the dumped.

At the root of this turmoil is the huge gap in his life where the person closest to him – his ex – used to be, the one around whom a large part of who he was revolved because he spent so much time with her and had so much emotion invested in their partnership. Take her away and there's a big blank space to fill.

A random warm female body won't plug that gap for anything longer than a night or two. Mere sex will treat the symptoms, not the cause. He needs time to adjust to the new circumstances and while the chances are he'll be beset by fear and insecurity every now and then, overall he may well relish his new-found freedom.

He will want to be *himself* for a change. He doesn't want to have to think about anyone else apart from himself for a while. He has time to *do* what he wants and *be* who he wants and if he has any sense at all he'll make the most of it.

But that freedom is not always great. Some men love being lone wolves for a change while others feel rudderless and lost. Every guy reacts differently and because we're as complicated as girls in many ways (and more complicated in some), predicting who will react in which way is impossible.

For women meeting men who are freshly out of relation-ships, the situation is far more straightforward: these guys should be avoided 99.9% of the time. In case you didn't get that the first time, I'll repeat myself: guys who are recently out of relationships should be avoided 99.9% of the time.

Why? Well, every day for these men is a potentially exciting step into the unknown and that sense of anticipation makes them dangerous. The unpredictability of their lives is what they relish most at moments like this. But if a guy doesn't know what he wants to be doing a week from now, how can he possibly be a good bet if you're looking for solid and secure dating potential?

That leaves any single girls who are still interested in one of these time bombs with one hell of a challenge, because unfortunately these men are extremely difficult to spot. There are very few obvious outward signs of their volatile state of mind for a girl to look out for.

For example, while some men will get new haircuts, new clothes and a taste for strippers when a relationship ends, others will settle for quietly changing their television viewing habits (out goes *Gossip Girl*, in comes *The Shield*) and that will be it. Some will want another girlfriend to stay at home with on Saturday nights as soon as possible while others will be determined to copulate casually with as many willing partners as they can find for the foreseeable future.

But soon afterwards the guy who wanted to sleep around at first might well decide he wants a new girlfriend while the guy who wanted a new relationship will get a season ticket to his local brothel instead. OK, that's a bit extreme, but you get the picture.

The tricky truth is that it's impossible to tell which category a newly single man is going to fall into until he has actually fallen and by then it's too late for the girl involved to look after herself. Hence the 99.9% I mentioned earlier.

Of course, that 0.01% does exist. In fact, I know one – a guy who ended a four-year relationship and then a week later got involved with someone else. Straight in he went, throwing all my tips and wisdom out of the window. And he was right to ignore me because they're now married and happy and it's a lovely, romantic story.

But don't let this freak occurrence fool you. I looked at a lot of people's romantic histories before writing this book and among them all this has only happened once.

One girl I know broke up with her ex at virtually the exact same time as a guy she had liked for a while finished his own relationship. They had a fling, she fell for him and for a while it was all late-night chats about fate's kindness and emotion-laden sex, while dreams of the future played out in her mind like cheesy movies.

But the dreams came crashing down because he quickly lost interest. For him, this near-relationship had come way too soon. He needed time on his own, time to be himself for a while. Which is why he was fine when the fling (that's all it was to him) ended. But she wasn't. The poor girl had completely lost control of the 'relationship' and ended up being hurt.

That, in a nutshell, is exactly the kind of situation I hope this book will help you avoid: the sort where your heart aches and you have no control over its fate.

Here's another example of a girl who could do with some straightforward advice about men who are *still* in relationships and why they should be avoided.

Inside the cheating mind

The following story surprised me in many ways, particularly as it came at a time when I hadn't been single for long and so was seeing the world through new eyes. One morning a girl sat down opposite me on the train into London. I'll call her Train Girl. She was not unattractive but not gorgeous and looked smart and tidy, like she was an accountant or a lawyer. And that's not meant as an insult.

Before I say any more, please do bear in mind that when this happened I hadn't been single for long, and while I knew girls were capable of treating men badly, I didn't realise they could be quite so vicious to *each other*. Yes, I was naïve. Perhaps because I'd never been the target of one of these girls.

Anyway, back to the story.

Train Girl's phone rang and she started a conversation about how she spent the previous evening. I had a book with me but like every other commuter in the carriage, her story was much more interesting than the one on the pages so I pretended to read and listened to her talk.

The girl had a great time, she said. The guy she met was flawless: funny, clever and rich. She definitely wanted to see him again. All good so far and a cheery conversation for a morning.

Then she went quiet while her friend spoke.

Her next words were these: 'Yes, I know he has a girlfriend. But I'm twenty-nine now and I'm single. Everyone else is hooked up already, so if I find a guy I like I'm going to go and get him if I can. And I like this guy.'

No hesitation and no sign of a conscience. Instead, there was steel in her voice. And a lot of raised eyebrows on that train.

I was staggered. I know I was naïve but I had no idea there was such a dog-eat-dog (or should that be bitch-eat-bitch?) spirit between females out there in the dating world.

I was never an angel but I like to think I wouldn't have deliberately moved in on another man's girlfriend. But then again, I was a thirty-year-old guy patiently ticking along in the single life, sure that the right girl was out there somewhere and that it was only a matter of time until I met her.

So I didn't think there was any reason for an attractive, single twenty-nine-year-old girl like the one on the train to panic about time running out, as this one appeared to be. But she clearly saw things differently.

What was on his mind?

There is absolutely no doubt whatsoever that the guy Train Girl was discussing was encouraging the flirtation. Things wouldn't have got this far if he wasn't.

So what was he up to? What was his endgame?

There were four possibilities. The first – and most innocent – was that he was simply having a flirt and reminding himself that he could still pull. Some men do this. That doesn't make it right, but it happens. It's as close to harmless as it's possible to get for him but for her, it's different and far more risky because she's the one who might get hurt when she finds out their flirting means nothing to him (he'll never leave his girlfriend for her).

Secondly, he might have been lining up Train Girl for a secret fling on the side. This is almost certain to also end badly for her.

Third, he might have seen her as a ready-made replacement for his current girlfriend, who he was going off, which makes him a Relationship Monkey (i.e. someone who doesn't leave their current boyfriend or girlfriend until the next one is ready and waiting – like a monkey swinging from one tree to another who won't let go of one branch until he knows which one he's going to grab hold of next). This is not very romantic and does not bode well for any relationship Train Girl might have with him, because the chances are he'd let go of her when he saw another tempting girlfriend/branch further down the line.

Finally, he might have had strong feelings for Train Girl that took him by surprise because he was happy with his girlfriend when they met. In this case it's possible – not likely, just possible – that he and Train Girl will end up happy ever after.

To be honest, I have no idea which one he was up to. But I do know that the chances of it being the last one – Train Girl's favourite – were slim. And the chances of the last one resulting in he and Train Girl being together and happy ever after are even slimmer.

How could Train Girl know what was on his mind? She couldn't. So what should she have done? Simple – avoid the guy who has a girlfriend.

What was on *her* mind?

My usual view of situations like this is that the guy involved is the predator and the girl is the victim. I know that's not always the case and girls aren't all that innocent but in my experience more often than not it's the man who wants to have his cake and eat it – in this case the cakes are his girlfriend plus another bit of romance, flirtation and/or sex. So this example seemed different because I had never heard of a girl behaving like such a predator before. I'm not saying it doesn't happen, just that I'd never heard of it.

In search of some female insight, I told a friend this story. She said Train Girl's behaviour was perfectly normal. I was shocked and said I'd never noticed such unladylike manhunting going on, let alone ever been on the end of it myself, and found it hard to understand.

'That's because you don't understand women,' she told me, before adding tantalisingly: 'There's only one thing you'll ever need to understand about women.'

Brilliant, I thought, this could be the nugget of information I've been waiting for since I had my first awkward encounter with a girl back when I was fourteen and tongue-tied by berserk hormones and sheer terror. Finally, everything was about to become clear. I was so excited I nearly spilt my coffee.

'It's this,' she said. 'The only thing you'll ever need to understand about women is that you'll never understand women.'

Sometimes I don't know why I bother.

Train Girl – conclusions

Train Girl thought she was being clever, I expect, but actually she was on the brink of getting herself in potentially painful emotional trouble because no matter how careful she tried to be, nothing she did would change which of the four possibilities was actually going on. Only one would be positive for her and the chances of it being that one were minimal. Not non-existent, just minimal.

I'm all for girls being proactive in clever ways in order to get guys but I cannot approve of using those tactics on guys who already have partners. Not because I object to the idea of trying to take away someone else's boyfriend or girlfriend but because the outcome is rarely happy for anyone. Not the boyfriend, the current girlfriend or the one trying to steal him.

That was a pretty strong statement I made in the last paragraph. I'd better explain.

If a guy tried to take Charlotte away from me, I wouldn't be happy. I'd probably want to punch him on the nose. Or worse. But if he was trying to take her away from me because he was helplessly in love with her, then I would understand why he did what he did. If he just wanted to seduce her then he could take a running jump off a very high cliff (and I might even give him a nudge to help him on his way). But where there's love involved, it's different. I don't think anyone can criticise another person for telling someone they're in love with them.

I also believe she wouldn't want to go off with him (unless he was Johnny Depp or, would you believe it, Bill Murray). But for the sake of argument, let's just say she did want to go, then it would probably be better for me and my long-term wellbeing if she did that sooner rather than later anyway.

That's a long-winded way of saying that all's fair in love and war.

Morality aside, just remember that if you're chasing someone already in a relationship, the one who's most likely to get hurt is you. Years ago, I learned a painful lesson about getting involved with a girl who was going out with someone else, because that was how the biggest heartbreak of my life came about.

About fifteen years back, long before I knew either Girlfriend

X or Y even existed and at a moment when I wasn't on the rebound from anyone else, this other girl and I had a little fling – quite an innocent one, actually, with lots of holding of hands and kissing and cuddling rather than explosions of passion – and after a couple of weeks I asked her to leave her boyfriend for me because I had fallen for her in a big way.

But she said no and I was devastated. I lost one of my closest friends and someone I thought I was in love with in one go. Quite a blow for a young man, I can tell you.

But I still went and did something very similar years later with The Big Mistake.

The Big Mistake – part one

I had a very good female friend who I used to go out with for drinks every now and then. We talked a lot and emailed regularly. She listened to me, was kind and generally lovely. As far as I was concerned, she didn't have a bad bone in her body. She was also very good looking.

She was just a friend, however, and she had a boyfriend who she lived with so nothing was ever going to happen. Ours was, for a long time, a completely platonic friendship.

I repeat: she had a boyfriend with whom she lived.

And that is one of the best possible reasons for not getting involved with someone. In fact, I'm struggling to think of any better ones, short of her being married with kids or a budding serial killer looking to make a name for herself by butchering single men.

But I was single and had a gap in my life marked 'Affection' and with her being so sweet to me, as she always was, we began to spend more and more time with each other. And she was really attractive, remember.

So I kissed her.

Which was, as I later realised, a big mistake.

But it took me a while to realise I was being stupid and a while for this girl to become The Big Mistake.

I was seeing The Big Mistake for about a month in total and generally things were romantic, illicit, exciting and passionate. And for the first few weeks, I didn't even think about her boyfriend. In my defence, I had never met the guy. Maybe if I had and could put a face and a voice to the idea of him, things might have been different. But I hadn't, so they weren't.

I know I was an idiot for getting involved with her but put yourself in my position, what was I supposed to do? *Not* make a move on this sexy, sweet and clearly willing girl who I was already close friends with? Actually, yes, that's precisely what I should have done. But life isn't that simple and decisions can't always be made that clinically. Especially when you're a single, red-blooded male in need of a kiss and a cuddle.

We had a good time in that month and I don't mind admitting I began to wonder if maybe our fling could turn into something more serious.

But soon after that it slowly began dawning on me that we were creating a huge and dangerous mess. A voice in my head said, 'Humfrey, there's no way anything serious and good between you can grow from a beginning like this. She's cheating on someone she's supposed to love. Do you want to be with someone like that? And you're encouraging her to go behind his back. Do you want to be that guy?'

The answer to both questions was no. But I ignored the voice.

Then I went out one night and met another girl. I didn't go out intending to pull but I spent the night with her and slowly my point of view on The Big Mistake began to change.

Why guys get lucky

Every guy knows very well that there are nights he gets lucky when he can take full credit for his success. Maybe it was a joke he cracked or the way he danced which made him irresistible. Or even his shirt. Could be a hundred different things.

But this night wasn't like that.

There are other times when a guy gets lucky and the one and only reason it happened was that the girl involved decided before she even stepped out of her front door that she was going out that night to get some action and he just happened to be the fortunate one.

I knew from the start that this was one of those nights. And I didn't care because it was only going to do me good, in much the same way as happened to a guy I know, who we'll call Jon.

The Affection Effect

A few months after Jon broke up with his long-term girlfriend, he spent the night with a former work colleague, a tall, blonde babe. At the time he was still only tentatively getting back into seeing other girls because he'd come out of that relationship feeling like shit. He'd been unhappy for a long time and because his ex made him feel like his life and feelings were insignificant little sideshows compared to hers, his confidence was some-where between zero and non-existent.

So when he was kissing this tall, blonde babe and opened his eyes to see her smiling, he was more than a little confused.

He broke off the kiss and asked her, 'Why are you smiling?' (not the coolest words a guy has ever come out with in the middle of a kiss).

'Don't girls always smile when you kiss them?' she said, still smiling.

And then she kissed him again.

Wow, he thought. Just, wow.

Nothing ever happened again between them after that night but if Jon had to single out one moment in those few months as the most significant in the recovery of his general wellbeing after the big break-up, that would be it. There was more physical warmth in that night than there had been in the previous couple of years and his enthusiasm for girls and life in general came flooding back.

Part of that was down to the fact a gorgeous girl was interested in Jon and his ego badly needed the boost, but most importantly, it reminded him of how utterly wonderful affection and intimacy are. Not just the sex, though. Jon meant the smiling, kissing and cuddling just as much, if not more.

The Big Mistake – part two

I didn't feel guilty about going behind The Big Mistake's back with this other girl because she was going home every night and sleeping in the same bed as her boyfriend. She told me they weren't still having sex, which I believed at first. But I soon realised that was exactly what she'd have said if they *were* still having sex. Given the web of lies and deceit we were creating I knew I couldn't believe her with any certainty at all so I didn't worry about it too much. I took what my friend Charlie calls the ostrich approach – I stuck my head in the sand.

Then she found out about this other girl and went crazy. Shouting, screaming, crying, the lot. Followed by a few hours where she wouldn't talk to me. Literally, wouldn't say a word. That was the moment when I realised The Big Mistake was The Big Mistake. A girl with a boyfriend was yelling at me – a single guy – for spending the night with a single girl. It was too ridiculous and complicated and at that moment I knew it would only get worse. Our fling had to finish.

I still regret getting involved with her because I lost a good friend (we could never go back to how things were) and the whole thing caused her a vast amount of heartache (certainly more than it caused me because she had guilt to cope with), which is why it was a big mistake.

How does a girl avoid becoming a rebound fling?

There are, contrary to what you might think after reading the last few pages, a couple of steps you can take to protect yourself. They are:

1. If a guy talks about a recent break-up and seems vulnerable and you start feeling like you want to look after him, run away. Chances are you'll nurse him back to emotional health, boost his confidence for a while and

then he'll look at you and think, 'Thanks for that, but I feel better now. I'm off to try my luck with some super-models. Goodbye.' That chance is 99.9%. I know of only one single example where this kind of rebound fling has become anything more significant. Only one.

2. If a guy talks about a recent break-up and seems completely together about it, run away. He's kidding himself and therefore kidding you too. See point 1 above for the relevant supporting stats.

I know at least some of you will ignore my previous two nuggets of wisdom, so if you really can't drag yourself away from him, there is another way to hedge your bets. It's called *talking*. Ask him honestly if he's ready for a new relationship. If he convinces you he is – I mean *really* convinces you, not just saying what's needed to get you into bed – then go for it. You have to gamble sometimes, remember.

But if it doesn't work out, don't say I didn't warn you.

Here's one more tip for luck: whichever of the two points above you ignore or pay attention to, in fact, whatever the situation you're in, don't rush into sleeping with the guy if you have any doubts about his state of mind or level of interest in you. Rebound sex for a guy is hugely cathartic – it wipes away his past and boosts his confidence for the future. Being the girl he has that rebound sex with is not so much fun because you are just a girl he's having sex with. The sex is all about him and his past and future, not you. So let him get that sex elsewhere.

And if after talking to him you realise you're not going to be his girlfriend, be content with being his friend.

The lesson

When I broke up with Girlfriend X I didn't want to go near another girl for months but when I broke up with Girlfriend Y I couldn't wait to start dating again. I was the same person both times and yet behaved completely differently. That is why men who have recently broken up with someone should be avoided. They are completely unpredictable and thus 100% unreliable. I include myself in that category. I am no different to any other guys.

It is also never, ever a good idea to either get involved with someone already in a relationship or to cheat if you're the one in the relationship. The older I get and the more I've seen and heard about these things going on, the more I am convinced that nothing good ever comes from infidelity.

Have I learned from The Big Mistake?

Yes. And I have not made the same mistake again.

(But I have made others.)

MEN SECRETS

The male ego is fragile and we like to feel we're attractive to girls.

There, I said it. My friends are going to kill me.

Men secrets

Sometimes guys can't help being made to do strange things by their emotions. You see, we're guys and guys are easily confused by emotions so our behaviour can become erratic. Weird, even. You should blame our emotions. We're not like that all the time.

Men sense:

1. Stay away from guys who are fresh out of relationships.
2. If your sixth sense tells you someone is on the rebound, they probably are.
3. If you feel like taking a risk on a guy who has just come out of a relationship, get to know him before anything physical happens.
4. Be aware that guys will almost definitely behave unpredictably. They can and will change their minds at any given moment for no apparent reason. THIS IS NOTHING TO DO WITH YOU.
5. Don't cheat and don't put up with cheats.
6. If things go wrong don't blame yourself. Guys are dumb. It was his fault.

Chapter Three

Getting Yourself Asked Out

- How to feel like a million dollars even when you're wracked with nerves
- Why men need to be directed towards asking you out
- How to appear reactive by being proactive – make him think he's making the moves
- Getting the balance right between being too forward and too cool

Picture the scene: you're out in public somewhere with a friend or two. Doesn't matter what time of day it is or where you are – it could be a party, a park or even a pound shop. The important bit is that you're in a place where there are people around who you don't know.

You see a guy and you like the look of him. The guy sees you and he likes you too. All good so far.

So, what next?

Assuming there's nothing in the background to stop him from approaching you (like you used to date his best mate or one of you isn't single), that guy will only shy away from talking to you or asking you out for one reason and one reason alone: fear of rejection. That, you see, is the biggest obstacle standing between single men and approaching girls they like.

The problem – and it is a problem – is that we're sometimes not very good at expressing our feelings.

I don't think there is one specific reason why this problem exists. My guess – as an amateur psychologist – is that it's a combination of the in-bred male conviction that all emotions are a little bit ridiculous, a view which stems partly from a lack of understanding. I mean, you can't see emotions, you can't smell them and you definitely can't touch them, can you? So what exactly *are* they? What do they look like? How do I know when I'm having one?

See what I mean? To the male mind it's all very confusing. Add in a possible genetic inclination to not show weakness (emotions are often classed as weakness in the male world) and things are even more complicated.

How to get a man to ask you out

That perspective is, I'm afraid, a fairly typical male one. But this does not need to be a major problem for you because with a few subtle moves you can make his insecurities and bred-from-the-cavemen defensive urges irrelevant. The way to do this is to control the whole meeting and dating process (the glorified mating ritual) in a way he doesn't even notice. The goal is to make him feel like *he* is the one who went out and got *you*, like he's the primitive hunter-gatherer we all want to be deep down, even when it was *you* who did the work.

To do this, you do not need to concern yourself with how a

guy boosts his own self-esteem (I'll explain all that later) and don't worry about the weird things he says to himself in the mirror before he goes out on the town. ('You're the honey. They're the bees,' is one example from a friend I won't name because I don't want to ruin his life.) Don't even think about how he might have rehearsed his opening line in his head before he's even left the house. And that does not mean you should follow *The Rules* (go back to page 23 if you need me to tell you why again).

Focus on what *you* can do.

And this is what that is.

The science of female flirting

I have a theory about how guys and girls make moves on each other. Note that phrase 'make moves on each other', because while guys are almost always the ones who lunge for that first kiss or suggest the initial date I believe it's girls who lead them by the hand into the right state of mind to be prepared to do this.

How?

Let's go all the way through the process, the modern-day mating ritual.

A guy sees a girl he likes. He feels a tingle inside which tells him he wants to make a move on her. Let's call this moment Point A. Think of it as the beginning of a journey. For the girl involved, if she likes the guy her goal is for him to reach Point B, which is the place where he actually gets up the courage to make his move, in other words the end of the journey (I'm assuming he's not one of those men who live their entire lives

51

at Point B – as I've already said, you should beware of them). The journey, then, is a simple one: from A to B.

Normal guys, those with average levels of confidence, need a little bit of help to get from Point A to Point B. The two points may be far apart or they may be close together; it depends on the guy and the girl. The point (different kind of point this time) is that there is distance between the points (back to the other kind of point) and it is the guy who needs to get from Point A to Point B.

If she's clever and wise, the girl can help him on his way with only a little bit of careful effort.

For example, a girl might hold eye contact for longer than a brief glance (one step along the journey). She might then smile at him (two steps) and if she's feeling brave she might even beckon him over (a short-cut to point B). He might then go and say hello to her, to which she responds in a friendly way (three steps) with more smiles. A few minutes later she might laugh at one of his stories (four steps). She might play with her hair (five steps). She might appreciate the way he asks her questions and listens to the answers before gently mocking her in an affectionate but not over-the-top way, resulting in her blushing a little bit while she smiles (six steps). By now they might be facing each other and he might suddenly realise she doesn't seem remotely interested in talking to anyone else except for him (seven steps). He might also realise that when she looks at him while he talks, she has tipped her head slightly and appears to be *really* listening to him (eight steps).

And on it goes until they have covered enough steps for him to feel he's reached Point B, where he will be brave enough to do something more substantial than hopeful flirting. If you make him feel good (i.e. make him believe that you think he's funny and interesting), he'll cover those steps more quickly and thus be more likely to make a move.

> ### Men secrets
> Making him feel good is the principle that underpins all the advice I'm going to give you about getting a guy you like to ask you out.

There is a limit, obviously, because throwing yourself at a guy is never a good idea (unless you want a quick roll in the hay and nothing else, in which case it's a very good idea) and I'll give you some examples of how not to do it later. For now, though, here are a few simple methods that can be used anywhere – a bar, a party, a library, DIY shop, *any*where:

1. **A smile goes a long way.** How many girls who don't look happy get approached by guys they like? Go on, have a guess. Any idea yet? That's right – none.

2. **Look like you're enjoying yourself.** This is linked to my previous point. Don't just grin like the Joker for no apparent reason (you'll look weird) but make sure you give the impression you're happy, even if you're doing something as uninspiring as buying picture hooks at the time.

3. **If someone looks at you, look back and smile** (there it is again). Don't hold eye contact for too long – you don't want to appear crazy – but don't look away immediately as if you've been caught doing something you shouldn't. There's the power of the smile again – if you look like

you're a happy and fun person, other people (including men) will want to be with you. Would you want to talk to someone who looks miserable? No, me neither.

4. **Do not ever doubt that you're attractive**. Ever. This is another nugget that you need to remember all the time. I don't have to see you to know that you're far more attractive than you think. Like just about every girl in the world, there will be things you don't like about your face or body. You will, if my experience is anything to go by, think these things dramatically undermine your general attractiveness. They don't. Trust me on that.

5. **Be confident**. Confidence is a funny thing. Until recently, I didn't understand what it was or where it came from. But now I do. Confidence comes from two places: how you perceive yourself and how others perceive you. And this is what I have concluded: if someone appears confident (just appears, it doesn't have to be real), they are treated as if they are confident by other people. If someone is treated as confident by others, that gives them confidence (the real stuff this time). So the trick is to begin by simply *appearing* confident and the rest will follow – others will perceive you as being more self-assured and in turn you will perceive yourself differently too. So how do you appear confident? In a nutshell, look like you're happy to be in the world and happy to be who you are and where you are. I'll say more on that subject in relation to dating later on but that is the foundation: appear happy and confident. Guys like being around girls who are happy and confident. It makes them feel good. And if you make them feel good, they like you.

But don't make him feel *too* good

If you try too hard to make him feel good (i.e. if you start treating him like he is the answer to the prayers of womankind), you'll come across as either desperate or easy. Or both. Unless it's a fling you're after, whether of the one-night variety or a little bit longer, these are not good impressions to give. Make him feel too good and he'll think he's too good for you.

The image you want to create is something like what Oscar Wilde was envisaging when he said: 'I don't say we ought to misbehave, but we should look as though we could.'

How to make him feel good but not too good

Be interested in him but a bit distant, which means that you shouldn't initiate physical contact, apart from maybe touching his arm once while he's talking to you. Let him do that. Talk and laugh as much as you want but keep physical contact to a minimum.

Don't be afraid to tease him. We love girls who give us a bit of banter. They are clever, entertaining and confident. And more importantly, most guys (at least, the ones who have senses of humour and don't take themselves too seriously) intrinsically understand the value of banter as a sign of affection. It's how we communicate with our friends and tell them we care. But don't be mean or nasty and always do it with a smile on your face.

If you're a happy and confident person (which you should be), you can make him like you by doing one simple thing: be yourself. Don't forget that.

How not to do it #1

If you see a guy at a bar, start talking to him and he offers you a drink, do not say, 'I don't want a drink, I want you to kiss me,' if you expect to be seen as anything other than a fling.

It happened to B and she turned out to be just a fling.

How not to do it #2

If you see a guy at a bar, start talking to him and he offers you a drink, do not say, 'I can't hear what you're saying, let's go back to my place,' if you expect to be seen as anything other than a fling.

It happened to B and, that's right, she turned out to be just a fling too.

How not to do it #3

If you see a guy at a bar, start talking to him and he offers you a drink, do not say, 'I don't feel like drinking. I feel like going home with you,' if you expect to be seen as anything other than a fling.

It happened to B and – you can probably guess what's coming next – she turned out to be just a fling.

DISCLAIMER:
All three of these girls may well have wanted no more than a fling, in which case good on them – their tactics worked perfectly and I respect their go-getting attitudes. I simply use their words as illustrations of how not to speak to a guy if you want more than a fling.

When, how and why you should ask a guy out

It is possible that even if you follow all my advice about men and flirting, the guy you like still won't ask you out. In this situation, assuming he doesn't have a wife or girlfriend, his reticence is almost certainly down to chronic shyness or a temporary lack of confidence. Under these circumstances you should not be afraid to make a less subtle first move.

That's right – *you* should ask *him* out.

But guys don't like that, I hear you say. It hurts their tiny, fragile male egos if they become the hunted rather than the hunter.

Wrong.

In fact, only some guys don't like being asked out and even that is only true some of the time.

And done the right way, asking out a guy who likes you but hasn't made a move is never, ever a bad idea.

So how do you do it the right way? First of all, you must bear in mind that a girl desperately chasing a guy isn't attractive, so you asking him out must be as subtle and non-pushy as possible. The move at the lowest end of the first-date pressure-building scale is simply to suggest going for a drink. That's all, just a drink. Not dinner, not the theatre, not the circus, not a day trip to Paris. Just a drink.

It's best to suggest it in the most low-key way you possibly can. An email or text saying, 'How about a drink next [insert day of the week]?' is enough. You should always specify a day and a venue, by the way, even if you end up going for another one, because at this stage you want to leave as few decisions to him as possible. And after all, men really don't care about first-date venues anyway.

Once he's said yes, treat the date like any other but with one more tip in mind: if you're on a date with a guy you've asked out, be especially wary about not sleeping with him too quickly. You've already told him you're interested by asking him out, so don't rush into taking things further – you don't need to make it any easier for him.

One more thing: even if you've had a conversation about, for example, a new film that you both really want to see or some other cultural event/activity of mutual interest and it subsequently struck you that a trip to the cinema/gallery/theatre/dog show might be a useful alternative to my 'just a drink' scenario, don't suggest it. That other kind of outing has 'friends' written all over it. My 'just a drink' plan is low-key, sure, but it's also unambiguously a date. You want to send a message, remember, and being subtle with men isn't a good idea.

Men who don't like being asked out

Generally it's the immature, insecure guys who don't like being asked out. Like me when I was sixteen, for example, when a girl

I knew slightly phoned me and asked if I wanted to go to the cinema with her. Being sixteen, I panicked because that wasn't what girls were *supposed* to do, and I said no. Had she made the same call ten years later, instead of being confused I would have respected her and almost certainly said yes purely on the grounds that I thought a girl asking a guy out was a cool thing to do.

To sum up: when I was sixteen I was immature and insecure but ten years later I wasn't. So that means asking a guy out will help you separate the immature and insecure boys from the grown-up guys.

The risks

For an explanation of the risks associated with asking a guy out, I will hand you over to B, who has this to say: 'I love it when a girl asks me out because she's putting it on a plate. I wouldn't disrespect a girl who asked me out but I would be more inclined to think she wasn't interested in anything serious. Obviously that would suit me just fine.'

So that's the risk – some guys (not all) will think you're a sure thing. The answer to this is, as I said above, if you want the date to turn into more than a fling, be especially cautious about how quickly things happen.

How to look like a million dollars even when you're wracked with nerves

Let's talk about confidence again. Look at point number four on page 54. The words that say: 'Do not ever doubt that you're attractive. Ever.'

This is the key. Unfortunately I can't make you do it.

Confidence and the newly single guy

While I was with Girlfriend Y, I was invited to a fashion awards party (it came through a work friend – then, as now, I knew nothing at all about fashion). My then girlfriend couldn't come so I invited a friend who had recently broken up with his girlfriend. Their relationship was dramatic in lots of unpleasant ways and ended with my friend, a good, decent guy, feeling emotionally battered and bruised, so I thought taking him to this party might be a laugh. At the very worst we'd have a night of drinks paid for by someone else.

The evening consisted of an awards ceremony followed by hours of drinks and music in a huge converted warehouse – a very trendy venue. We arrived a few minutes before the awards started and were immediately faced with a choice between watching a load of people we'd never heard of get awards for things we didn't understand or care about (my friend wasn't into fashion either) or getting comfortable at the free bar in the main party room next door.

This was not a difficult decision.

We spent the next hour necking drinks and waiting for the ceremony to finish. Eventually the other guests began trickling in. This being a fashion party, there were loads of extremely hot women around so we were very happy just chatting away and admiring the female scenery as they milled around us, all immaculately presented and fragrant.

But after a few minutes of looking around something unpleasant clicked in my mind: I realised we were easily the least trendy men in the place. I began to feel a little self-conscious. Soon after that we noticed people were staring at us and I began to feel genuinely uncomfortable.

Maybe this wasn't such a good idea after all, I thought, because in a crowd of several hundred people we were feeling like fish out of water. We found it impossible to blend in among the trendy fashion guys who as well as being dressed differently to us, all seem to be skinny and average height at best, unlike both of us who are very tall and physically more solid than elegant. Bringing my friend to this party was, I feared, about to do him more harm than good.

Then odd things started happening. First, a couple of girls asked us to dance with them. We dismissed that as a freak occurrence.

Soon after that, two more came along to say hello and started chatting to us. After they went off to the bar, three more appeared. And then another one on her own.

It took a woman coming up and demanding that we 'stop torturing all the girls in here and start dancing' for the penny to drop: we were just about the only non-fashion-victim straight men in the place and stood out like sore thumbs. In those surroundings – a party where everyone has made an effort to look good and is out for a fun time – the effect was spectacular. The next few hours saw the most extraordinary level of female attention I have ever known and, I suspect, ever will. I lost count of the number of women who approached us. One even came up to me and said: 'I'm going home in ten minutes and I want you with me,' while my friend was on the receiving end of all kinds of filthy propositions (more than me, I'm sorry to say).

My friend decided early on not to accept any of these offers (his first 'Come home with me now' invitation came at about 11 p.m. when we'd only been there for an hour) because it seemed a shame to cut this unique event short. This led to us having a night that neither of us will ever forget.

Kicking out time was 5 a.m. and we stayed until the bitter end, spending the last hour dancing in the middle of a group of random girls. I'm a terrible dancer (I really am, I'm not being modest) but these girls reacted like they'd just been released from an all-women prison and suddenly had twin Justin Timberlakes cutting shapes in their midst.

At 5 a.m. we staggered to the twenty-four-hour bagel joint on Brick Lane, laughing our heads off and not quite able to believe what had just happened to us. What a night. What a brilliant, magic night.

As for my intention to cheer my friend up, it worked a treat. He was walking on air afterwards, not least because he had about fifteen girls' business cards in his pocket. I don't think he ever called any of them but that wasn't the point. The night had served its purpose: he felt attractive again.

Years on, we still laugh about that night. And we were right about one thing – nothing like that has happened since. That night was unrepeatable, one where the stars aligned in our favour for one unique evening the likes of which we will never see again.

And do you know what? I don't mind that it was a one-off. These days playing the field doesn't matter to me and as long as I have my memories, I'm happy. Unlike B, who nearly exploded with rage when I told him what he'd missed out on.

Quiet times – getting through a dry spell

Ah yes, confidence. Here is the beginning of the most ego-destroying period of my single life. The one in which my confidence all but vanished.

About nine months after I became single I was in a slow period dating-wise. I say slow rather than dry because I wasn't all that bothered about not meeting girls at the time so the lack of action didn't worry me. Being single was fine. It was my choice.

At least it was at that moment. Little did I know that I was witnessing the dawn of the single man's worst nightmare: a dry spell. A month later the situation was getting worse. I hadn't had so much as a kiss on the cheek for weeks and weeks. But there was a light at the end of the tunnel: I was going to a wedding.

Weddings are meant to be fertile pulling grounds for singles. All those emotions, all that alcohol and all those beautifully dressed guests should, in theory at least, blend to form a powerful cocktail of romantic urges.

So I was hoping for great things from this one. It was a gorgeous winter wedding and the day was brilliant – a lovely location just outside London, a truly happy couple, lots of friends there and the tone was set by the funniest first dance I've ever seen: a deliberately cheesey, choreographed routine performed to Lionel Richie's 'All Night Long' – absolute magic. Plus the booze started flowing at about 3 p.m. so there was plenty of time for spirits to soar.

But there was a problem: no single girls, which meant all the romance in the air went to waste. For me, anyway.

At dinner, the two women next to me both had their partners on their other sides, a husband to my left and a fiancé to my right. The engaged couple had just been reunited after a few weeks apart, so understandably had little interest in anything other than kissing each other, which I didn't find depressing at all. Not in the slightest. Really I didn't.

OK, I wanted to throw a drink over them. But I managed to control myself.

Luckily, the woman on my left was great company and we chatted about lots of different things, including her husband going to the same school as me. Or at least we did until my friends at the next table (a table of five couples, by the way) spotted me talking to her and leapt to the hugely mistaken conclusion that she was single and on the receiving end of a charm offensive from me.

They then did what any supportive, kind and helpful set of friends should do (and probably what I'd have done in their situation): they started heckling me.

'Humf, are you winning?' my friend Josh shouted repeatedly.

No Josh, I thought to myself, I'm not winning. In fact I'm not even in the game. And there was worse to come.

'Has he started talking to you in French yet?' yelled Nick.

No, I hadn't done that either, not least because she was actually French (I speak French but not like a native so she wouldn't have been impressed). And let's not forget she was married anyway. In the end I asked her to hold up her left hand to shut them up.

Painful as my so-called friends were, it was a great day. And I did find a positive angle on the irritation of being single at that wedding: I was much happier single than I was as part of one of those couples who hears nothing but 'When's it going to be you?' all day.

At this wedding my view was simple: give me no pressure every time.

But at this wedding I hadn't met anyone I wanted to marry.

MEN SECRETS

At the 'meeting' stage, single men are not complicated because our confidence is not always straightforwardly strong. Make them feel good and it's half the battle won.

The art of female flirting (badly)

We've established that girls can over-flirt so much they put a guy off. They can also under-flirt, which means not doing enough to get the guy to move from Point A to Point B.

For example, I knew a girl at university who I thought a lot of. She was fun, we had a laugh and were great friends. We studied together and hung out, despite having very few friends in common (being a London girl she was much, much cooler than me, a boy from quiet, little Cambridge).

She was also attractive but I'd never even contemplated thinking about her in that way because not only was she much cooler than me but I knew she only ever dated black guys. I found out that her taste in men was set in stone just after we met and briefly thought, 'That's a shame for me,' but after that moment she was only ever a friend to me. In my mind the idea of being with her romantically was a total non-starter so thoughts on the subject never arose and it didn't bother me because I'd known from virtually day one that nothing was ever going to happen. Even Brad Pitt wouldn't have stood a chance with her, I thought.

Eventually we started spending less time together and when we left university we lost contact. A few years later I bumped into a friend of hers who I hadn't seen for a long, long time. I asked after my old friend and the girl told me her news. Then she said: 'It's a shame you two never got together.'

I laughed and said something about it not really being an option because I wasn't her type.

The girl looked at me. 'What do you mean, not her type? She really, really liked you. Why do you think she came to see you all the time?'

Now that was a surprise. I honestly had no idea she was even remotely interested in me as anything other than a buddy. None at all. I was, after all, neither cool nor black.

There are two ways of looking at this. Either a) it's a shame nothing happened because we got on so well and so a relationship could have been great or b) it doesn't matter that she was interested in me because I obviously didn't feel the same. Regardless of what her 'type' was, I would have known if I'd had feelings for her (though whether I'd have acted on them is another matter entirely).

On the balance of probability and knowing what I was like back then (still a boy in a lot of ways), b) is probably true and I wasn't interested enough in her. But the lesson is this: if she really did like me as more than a friend, wouldn't it have been better for all concerned if I'd known about it? If she really was interested in me, she would have found out definitively if I liked her too. If I did, great, and if I didn't she could forget about me.

You remember I said earlier that girls need to lead guys they like by the hand into a state of mind where they have the confidence to make a move? Well, this is an example of how not to do it. Was I being too harsh on the girl I knew at university? Maybe. The thing is, assuming she was actually interested in me, I suspect she was suffering from the same affliction that stops men from asking girls out: she was afraid of rejection.

On the upside, this is something men and women have in common – I've bottled out of telling girls I liked them too.

We're not so different after all.

How a guy missed his chance (he was stuck at Point A)

A friend of mine liked a guy for about a year. She knew him through work and they saw each other regularly. She thought there was something brewing up between them but he didn't say or do anything.

One night, he brought his new girlfriend to a party where my friend was. Being a good person, my friend told him she thought the girlfriend was nice and he'd done well for himself. He said thank you but then paused and added something along the lines of: 'I only started seeing her because I didn't think you were interested.'

This is what my friend thought of that: 'Why couldn't he have grown a pair of balls and told me? He had a year to do it! Until that moment, I liked him too. But after that I thought he was weak and pathetic and I was over him immediately.'

Harsh but fair, you're probably thinking. Well, maybe. But I'm going to defend the poor chap anyway.

He obviously really liked my friend. He hung out with her and they spent a lot of time together. He'll have thought about her far more than she realised. Every time he was with her, he'd have been imagining her as his girlfriend. I don't mean he would have been picturing her naked all the time (only some of it). Instead, images of them doing boyfriend-and-girlfriend-type things would have played in his mind, walking in a park on a sunny day or cuddled up on a sofa. He would have liked her so much he could see something serious developing between them and as soon as a guy feels like that, he's on dangerous territory because suddenly there's a huge amount at stake. That's when the fear can strike. And it's that fear which sometimes gets a guy stuck at Point A.

OK, that's not much of a defence. I've explained his behaviour but I can't justify it, not even to myself. I admit it – he should have grown a pair of balls and told her how he felt.

Sometimes guys are useless.

But she was useless too, because if she'd told him how she felt, things might have been different.

And remember, you're better off with a guy who's stuck at Point A and needs a nudge to make a move, than one who lives his entire life at Point B, like B.

How B became a guy who lives at Point B

When B was about twelve, he went to a disco at his school. It was one of those where all the parents came along as well and B's much older brother (at least twelve years older and earning his own money) decided the evening was going to be pivotal in the boy's development. B was the right age to learn a lesson he would never forget.

And so he did, because that night B's brother told him that every time he asked a girl to dance he would give him five pounds. It didn't matter if she said yes or no, he just had to ask. Bear in mind B was twelve at the time and this was about twenty years ago, so five pounds was *a lot* of money. Being a relatively bright chap, B figured out very quickly that the embarrassment of being turned down by a girl was a price well worth paying for those five pounds and so he spent the evening asking girl after girl to dance. Of course, some said no. But some said yes, and by the end of the night he'd danced with lots of girls and earned himself an almost unthinkable amount of money.

The lesson was this: being turned down doesn't matter. And B's fear of being rejected by a girl was never seen again.

Lucky, lucky man.

The consequences, or reaping the whirlwind

Thus B became the stereotypical guy who lives his entire life at Point B (B is for Point B and Bad Boy, by the way). The kind of guy who will see an attractive girl, go up to her and say something like, 'Nice shoes. What's your name?' or, 'You're gorgeous. Fancy a drink?' and if she shows no interest at all, will think nothing of it and simply start looking for the next unsuspecting female to appear.

I warn you again: if a guy is too smooth and seems almost ridiculously confident, you're not special. You're just another girl in his sights.

Where you find these men

Everywhere.

MEN SENSE:

1. Don't ever doubt that men find you attractive.
2. If you want to be approached, look approachable. That means smile.
3. Beware of guys who seem too relaxed and confident about approaching you.
4. Do not rule out the ones who seem a bit shy and not quite so smooth.
5. If you like someone, tell them. You're much better off knowing they're not interested than torturing yourself by wondering if they are.

Chapter Four

The First-Date Minefield

- How to arrange a first date
- How to arrive at a first date
- What to talk about on a first date
- How to end a first date
- Blind dates
- Online dating

Dating again after breaking up with Girlfriend Y was a daunting prospect. Years had passed since I was last in a potentially romantic situation with a girl I barely knew. That's why the first dates I had immediately after becoming single were with girls who weren't strangers. Those flirtations didn't exactly turn out brilliantly and so for a while afterwards I didn't do much dating at all.

Why? What was I afraid of?

Humfrey Hunter

The single man's fear

It wasn't the idea of being with a girl in a social situation that worried me. But the prospect of being alone with a *new* girl in a situation where we'd have to talk to each other didn't fill me with joy.

At the time I was confused and retreated into my shell a bit. Looking back I understand much better now what was going on in my head. I was in that period of adjustment that follows a break-up, that time when you rebuild yourself and your life, and I wasn't sure yet how well I was doing or how successful my rebuilding would be.

At that stage, the idea of being under examination by a girl who viewed me as a potential boyfriend was scarier than any job interview I could remember. I imagined how my life (my work, my friends, even my bedroom) would look seen through her eyes and in my mind I only saw the weak points (not much money; beer drinkers with a childish sense of humour; very messy). It didn't fill me with confidence.

First dates started to feel like some kind of exam or job interview. My mind was full of questions. What if she didn't like me? What if she thought my jokes were stupid and immature rather than funny and playful? What if she thought my determination to follow my dream career rather than go corporate and chase money was the result of my stubborn refusal to grow up instead of a positive character trait?

And – here's the big one – what if she didn't fancy me?

That would be a *disaster*.

So my first First Date was a big moment. There would be nowhere to hide. I would have to confront my fears. I would have to push my insecurities down deep inside, away from

72

prying female eyes. And when the time came, I even had to convince myself she wasn't just seeing me for a joke.

OK, I'm exaggerating now. I wasn't as nervous as all that. I was only a little bit nervous. And those nerves happened because that first date meant something. If I'd averaged three first dates a week for the past couple of months I would have been fine. But that one was a milestone, my *first* First Date for years.

So how did it go?

Fine, actually. There's no need to bore you with the details (it was completely unremarkable – I met a girl out one night, took her number and had a few drinks with her a week later and that's it). All you need to know is that I managed to not mess it up and I achieved this by doing two simple things: asking questions and listening to the answers. Basic social skills, really. Funny how they come in handy sometimes. As do a few glasses of wine.

But that's not the interesting part. The interesting part came next.

Because my luck had to change sooner or later. And eventually (a couple of months later), I managed to get a girl to go out with me.

First, let me fill in the background.

There's no accounting for taste (especially mine)

The longer my dry spell went on (I don't want to dwell on those months but they were without doubt a fully fledged dry spell), the more of an interest my friends took in my love life. By now the question I was asked more often than any other was, 'What exactly are you looking for?' And it's one I could never give a decent answer to.

You see, some guys go for the same kind of girl time after time after time. Whether it's hair colour, height, personality or even her job, there is often a strong pattern in men's dating histories. And, of course, the same is true for many girls who are repeatedly attracted to the same kind of guy.

But it absolutely isn't the case for me. I don't have a type at all and I never have. In theory, this is great as it makes my female target range absolutely vast – i.e. all of them. However, the truth is it causes problems because I never knew what I was looking for in a girlfriend, except for obvious qualities like beautiful, funny, kind, passionate (which, by the way, is a polite euphemism for 'loves sex', no matter who says it), clever, happy, doesn't take herself too seriously, loves food and is able to understand that my lack of tidiness is quirky rather than annoying.

Aside from that, I'd struggle to come up with anything else. Hair colour? Don't care. Job? Doesn't bother me. Age? Within reason (i.e. not so young as to be immoral and not so old that her child-producing years are history), I'm not fussed. So where did that leave me? Spoilt for choice? No, just bewildered.

The heights of attraction

A friend of mine, Rob, is 6' 5" and can't control himself around loftier ladies. In fact, he was once so overcome with lust at the sight of a girl just an inch shorter than him in a pub that his opening line to her – delivered in the same tone as a guy would say 'You're the most beautiful girl I've ever seen' when he really, *really* means it – was 'Oh my God, you're *massive!*'

Unsurprisingly, she didn't take it as a compliment, even though it was meant as one, and all he got was a slap.

But my taste is different. I'm 6' 4" so only a tiny bit less tall than Rob but I quite like the feeling I get with girls who are smaller than me. Makes me feel like a man.

Obviously when you can stand up straight and still be nose-to-nose with a girl you don't get that feeling. As a result, the tallest woman I've ever dated was 5' 10" (which isn't tall compared to me) and my dry spell may well have ended much sooner if I hadn't been so determined to stick to my ways.

The near miss

I was in a club when a very cute girl of average height (through my drunken eyes she looked like Holly Willoughby) came up to me and said: 'Hi, I'm Annie.'

For a split second I thought I'd won the pulling lottery – a gorgeous girl had made the first move. But then came the kicker. 'And this is my friend, Jo,' she said, turning to introduce me to a second girl who loomed behind her in an obvious my-friend-is-only-saying-hello-to-introduce-me-to-you way.

Jo was, in Rob's own words, *massive*. Slender and pretty as well, but still massive. She must have been about 6' 2" and with heels (she was wearing heels, I checked) her eyes were at the same level as mine. Jo might have ticked every other box I can think of (funny, clever, kind, thinks my untidiness is endearing, etc. etc.) but it wouldn't matter. She was too tall and being made to feel small is not sexy for me.

And anyway, her friend was gorgeous so, cruel as it might sound, that was where I focused my efforts.

Eventually, it paid off. I was only really talking to Annie and soon Jo began chatting to someone else. Annie was very funny and sweet and when Jo came to get her because her group was leaving, I asked for her number. Annie made sure Jo was out of sight and gave it to me.

Did I feel bad for not giving Tall Jo a chance? Not then I didn't. But by the end of my first and only date with Annie I knew I'd picked the wrong girl.

NOTE #1:

I told this story in my column and the feedback was extraordinary. I was called all kinds of things for the sin of rejecting Too Tall Jo. Weak, spineless, chauvinist, sexist were only a few. I mean, seriously? So I don't fancy tall girls, what's the big deal? Does that make me a bad person? No. Can anyone explain that to me?

NOTE #2:

Yes, it turns out someone can explain that to me. I showed Note #1 to my friend Lucy and she said this: 'Let me enlighten you on the virulent response to your rejection of Too Tall Jo. The pool of men for women who are taller than 6ft is very small indeed. Just as it helps you feel manly being taller than your woman, tall girls aspire to be with someone even taller than themselves, in order to feel feminine (not an easy feat when you tower above most people). The letters you got were from women who were dismayed to find that even if they do find a really tall, attractive man (rare), they still have almost no chance against 'normal' women. You're effectively saying these women are completely screwed. I know this because I have a friend who's over 6ft, and 'tall' is the number one item on her wish list, and because even I, at a paltry 5"8, find it difficult to find guys I like who are significantly taller than me. I'm currently dating someone who's 5"9 and if there was one thing I could change about him . . . yep, you guessed it.'

All that feedback makes sense now. If I was a tall girl I wouldn't have been pleased either, so that's me told. And for what it's worth, I know a guy who is 6'2 and married to a girl who's 6'1, only an inch shorter – or less tall – than him so, Lucy, all is not lost. Just because I don't fancy tall girls doesn't mean plenty of other men won't find them irresistible.

Annie the Facebook stalker, or why you should play it cool

I called Annie a couple of days later and asked if she wanted to meet for a drink. She did. And a couple of days after that we were sitting in a bar in Covent Garden throwing cocktails down our necks.

She wasn't quite as cute as I remembered (only Holly Willoughby really looks like Holly Willoughby) but she was funny and the signs were all good. Then we started talking about Facebook and the can of worms opened.

Rewind a couple of days to after I'd asked her out but before our first date and Annie tracked me down and poked me – a mildly flirtatious gesture that made me smile. I poked her back a few hours later and that was that.

Or at least I thought it was.

When we mentioned Facebook, she unleashed an alarmingly detailed critique on what my profile said about me, including thoughts on all the photos that are on my page and, worst of all, an analysis of how we knew some of the same people. 'How do you know him?' she gabbled, 'I met her there. What about him? He used to date my best friend. That other one's a friend of my cousin. How weird!'

Err, not really.

London isn't actually that big a place when you work in the media and are older than about twenty-one (Annie was twenty-eight) so this was slightly unnerving.

I'd dated girls before who I knew through mutual friends and in those circumstances you accept there is common social ground between you. But when it was someone I thought was a total stranger, suddenly finding out she knew much more about me than I thought felt like she was intruding. I lost interest in her quickly. Like in a couple of minutes. Frankly, I thought she was a bit weird.

Now Facebook is here, your private life really isn't that private at all if someone can know that much about you so easily. Bear in mind this happened a couple of years ago, during the earlyish period of Facebook when no one really thought too deeply about what it meant or how to use it in a dating context. For me, this was a watershed moment and afterwards I viewed Facebook differently.

The craziest of the crazy

There are two things you need to remember about crazy behaviour, which are true whether the behaviour is committed by guys or girls. First, if you're drunk it doesn't count, and second, no matter how extreme the most bonkers thing you've ever done might be, someone else has done something madder.

Like the girl a nameless friend of mine dated, for example. Here's the story:

'I went out for a few weeks with a very highly strung girl. She was what I'd call kooky or artsy and I liked that. Then I realised she was beyond kooky/artsy. She was mad.

'When did I realise this? It might have been when she got the idea that I was cooling off on her (I hadn't been until . . .) and started stealing essential items from my flat every time she came over. I'd notice when she'd gone that my rail season ticket was missing. Then my passport. Next time all my knives and forks. Then my work shoes. Then my camera. My current reading. My socks. My kettle.

'Each time this happened I'd ring her and ask: "Did you, um, take all my knives and forks/passport/whatever when you were over earlier?" and she'd laugh forcedly and a bit too loudly and deny it. I told her I knew she had. She'd then (yup, always the same) laugh a bit too forcedly and loudly and go, "Good heavens, that must have slipped into my bag," or, "Sorry, I thought it was mine."

'One day I caught her sneaking my kettle into her bag and she broke down and said she knew I was planning to ditch her and stealing these essential items was the only way she could be certain I'd need to call her again.

'I cooled off then for sure. And a few weeks later, I left the house in the morning and noticed fluttering paper on my neighbour's door. And my neighbour's neighbour's door. And my neighbour's neighbour's neighbour's door. In fact, all up and down my road, I mean sixty houses or more, front doors had handwritten letters pinned to them denouncing me for being a bastard. In her hand. With silver pen-drawn stars and moons all over them.

'She called the next day and asked if I wanted to come on holiday with her.'

That is off-the-charts crazy. I know that because I canvassed some friends to see if anyone could beat that. They couldn't but there were some more than mildly bonkers runners-up. Here are the best five slightly loony ladies:

1. The girl who accused her boyfriend of having an incestuous relationship with his sister because that sister called him 'babes'. The fact she called everyone else 'babes', *including the girlfriend*, didn't matter.
2. The girl who phoned the parents of her boyfriend of two weeks to tell them she thought he'd died in a car crash because she hadn't heard from him since he went to play golf . . . two hours earlier.
3. The girl who insisted a guy she was dating tip his head forward when he looked at her so she couldn't see his nostrils . . . because she had a phobia of nostrils.
4. The girl who on the first date with a guy she barely knew told him she'd had a premonition of them together aged eighty.
5. The girl who was dumped by a guy after a month (no cheating or anything bad, it just wasn't working) and

tried to win him back by leaving ten cans of carrot soup on his doorstep. He'd mentioned he liked carrot soup. Once.

Finally, here's one to even up the score – a story where the guy and girl involved both went bonkers. This extraordinary tale is reproduced below exactly as it was told to me by one of my friends about a friend of his:

My friend, let's call him Joe, is a reasonable man. Keeps himself to himself, a normal guy. Except when it comes to women. He makes monumentally bad decisions on the spur of the moment – and none worse than his decision to fly 3,000 miles to Canada to hook up with a woman he'd met two weeks before. On Facebook. And spoken to on the phone. Once. For twelve minutes.

He was due to stay with her in Vancouver for two weeks. Three days in, however, Joe realised she wasn't quite the girl of his dreams. She locked him in her house each day when she went to work, even bolting the windows in case he tried to – in her own word – 'escape'. Then she'd ask him when he was planning to propose.

Unable to afford an earlier flight home, Joe decided to stick it out for the fortnight. Three days before he was due to fly, however, she went completely off the rails after he said he didn't love her. After ranting and raving at him, she literally took his luggage and slung it into the street, refusing to allow him back in. Now, Joe was in a desperate state. He'd maxxed out his credit card for the last-minute round-trip and had left what little cash he had in his wallet, which was still inside the woman's house. With the woman refusing to answer his calls, Joe was forced to pay for a taxi to the airport and use his mobile as collateral. Once at the airport, he again tried the woman. *She answered and came to the airport. Joe was relieved, thinking that she'd come to her senses and would let him sleep at hers.*

Instead she had a bag in her hand. 'Your dirty laundry,' she said.

Then she left.

Despite his repeated pleas, the woman refused to answer Joe and help him out. He had three dollars to live on for three days and bought himself two Mars bars for food and a box of baby wipes to wash with in the men's toilets.

Three excruciating days later, he was back in London.

'Last time I ever fly halfway around the world on a first date,' he told me.

'Lesson learned.'

Wow.

'It's not stalking, it's research'

Remember how I keep pointing out the way men behave differently under identical circumstances with different girls? Well, fast forward two years and here's another example.

After we'd been dating for a while, not long, just a few weeks, Charlotte told me that just after we met she Googled me and put my name into Facebook and, unlike how I felt with Annie, this didn't bother me at all. Not one bit. In fact I was quite pleased she'd wanted to find out more about me.

Naturally I teased her a bit and jokingly called her a stalker (I didn't mention that I'd done exactly the same thing with her name) to which she said: 'It's not stalking, it's research.' Which I think is a very wise comment. Of course you want to know more about the person you're dating. It's perfectly natural. So what she and I both did was research, not stalking. I'm happy with that.

The lesson, then, is to keep your research under your hat, at least until you've been seeing the person long enough for revelations like that not to matter. Whatever you do, absolutely do *not* do as Annie did and mention it on your first date.

That's when plain, innocent research really does feel like stalking.

Don't be a stalker. It's not clever.

Now back to my single years.

The interesting part

The interesting part is what came after that very first First Date. You see, guys aren't always nervous before first dates. I was that time but the more I went on, the easier they became. I don't mean I went on hundreds before the penny dropped. Rather, after a handful I realised what it was I needed to do to make sure I had a good time. And that was this: look at the date as a chance to have a fun evening and that's it. Nothing else.

That meant shutting out the two main questions on a guy's mind during an enjoyable first date, namely whether or not he is going to get laid at the end of it and if a second date is on the agenda. I realised that if I liked a girl enough to want to spend an evening with her (note that was an *evening*, not a night) then I should view it as just that – an evening with her – and try to have fun on that limited basis.

All past experiences, good and bad, were irrelevant, as were hopes for the future. The First Date thus becomes a self-contained bubble to be enjoyed for what it is and absolutely nothing more. Not for what it might or might not be at some unknown point in the future, but for what it is.

One evening of entertainment.

If it went well, then I could start thinking about what might happen later that night or the second date. Until then, focus on the first. That way, the pressure came off and I was free to enjoy the evening as simply a fun event. Not a process or the beginning of anything. But just an event.

The Male Dating Cycle

The approach I've just described is not the one taken by all single men. It applies only to those who are not interested in commitment (something these guys themselves might not realise). In my case, by treating dates as one-offs rather than openings to a potential relationship, I cut myself off from the possibility of getting truly involved with anyone. With the benefit of hindsight, it's obvious I was subconsciously putting up barriers. I compare these dates to the first time I went out with the girl I'm now living with and my mindset was completely different. Back then it was: 'This could be fun for an evening or even two.' But when I met Charlotte, even before our first date I was excited and thought, 'Something serious might be starting here.' There was no pre-planned limit to what might develop.

Until a guy reaches the stage where he is ready for a girlfriend – the one I reached with Charlotte – he goes through what I call 'The Male Dating Cycle'.

What is The Male Dating Cycle?

Look at this graph:

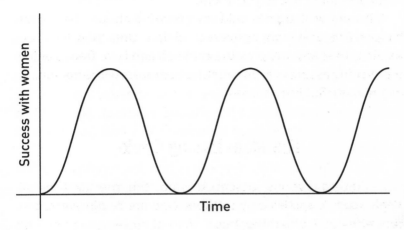

This illustration shows the ups and downs of a single man's dating life. The up is when he is on fire, pulling girls with ease and generally feeling unstoppable (this does not necessarily mean he's actually seeing lots of girls – that depends on the guy – how he feels is what matters). The bottom of the graph is when he hasn't had a date, let alone sex, for months. A single man's life travels roughly along this line, following the pattern of ups followed by downs followed by ups followed by downs – hence me calling it The Male Dating Cycle (I expect there's a female one too that looks remarkably similar).

It's important to note that when a guy becomes single, he can join the line anywhere between the top and bottom. Precisely where depends on the guy. Let's say, for example, he joins bang in the middle. He's not feeling very confident because it's been a while since he was last single but gradually he gets into the swing of things. He remembers how it works and realises that now he's a bit older, the game is easier to play. Slowly but surely he gets better at dating until he reaches the top.

But after a while the top gets boring. Too easy. He realises he's not looking for anything serious and becomes less interested in dating for the sake of dating, so he takes a break from girls. He pulls back and stops dating completely. For a while this is fine. He knows why he isn't meeting any girls (he isn't trying) and he feels a bit virtuous as a result because he's not leading any girls on or behaving like a bad boy. He feels civilised and in control.

This feeling can last a few weeks or a few months. The first sign that it's cracking is when he says to himself, 'It's been a while . . .' Initially he laughs off that thought. Being a non-dater was his choice, after all. But as that voice comes more often his doubts begin to grow. Memories of the last girls he dated fade and sooner or later he no longer feels like the guy who had girls at his fingertips.

He stops thinking, 'I don't want to pull.' He moves on to, 'I haven't pulled for a while,' before graduating to, 'I hope I can still remember how to pull.' Finally he ends up at the bottom of the curve, a sad, lonely place where a single guy is convinced he can't pull any more and in all likelihood never will again. This is not a fun time in a man's life.

For some guys this drought doesn't last long. For others the dark period can last forever, or a few years, at least until a girl shows an interest in him (in which case he will be so grateful that a girl – any girl – likes him that he'll probably propose to her six months later out of fear that she'll change her mind and leave him).

But for those guys who manage to break away from the bottom of the cycle, the impact is dramatic. As soon as the single guy pulls again he rockets up to the top. Confidence comes flooding back and away he goes, pulling all the time until he decides a few weeks or months later that it's getting boring and he wants to opt out for a while. You can guess what happens next: on it goes until he's finally ready for a Proper Girlfriend, a moment which can also happen at any point in the cycle.

You've already heard about my time at the bottom of the cycle, so let's get back to first dates.

The pre-first date ritual

The period between meeting a guy and him asking you out is horrible. A combination of no-man's-land, limbo and purgatory, this is not a place where people like to be. And you think a guy doesn't feel the same, right? Wrong.

When a guy meets a girl he really likes, he wants to know as soon as possible when he's going to see her again. He wants a date locked in to her diary so he knows he's going to have the opportunity to make her his before anyone else does.

Pre-date texts and how to interpret them

I'll cover this subject briefly here because there's more detail on the subject in the next chapter. Basically, this is how to do it: if he texts you, reply an hour later at first and then more quickly according to how he does it. The golden rule is never reply quicker than he does but never leave it too long either. (I hate those games.)

If you don't hear from him and are wondering if he's actually interested in seeing you, either assume he's not bothered and move on, or text him once and if he doesn't reply in two hours then give up on him. The general rule is that if he doesn't text you, he's not interested. If he's not trying to see you, then he's not bothered.

When I met Charlotte, I texted her the next day and didn't even attempt to play it cool. My theory was that if two people like each other, all they both want is to hear from the other and meet up. As long as that's accomplished, it doesn't matter who texts who when. But don't deliberately take ages because that's just rubbish. Playing it that cool – unless he's a player too – is not good for anyone.

And remember that some men – only a very few – will do the 'don't call for three days after you meet her' thing as well because they don't want to seem too keen. This is a slightly different scenario to a guy who doesn't reply to one of your texts because he doesn't like you, but the assumption you should make about him – that he's not all that interested in you – is the same. Why? The three-days guy is following a pre-planned set of rules and guys who really like a girl don't do that, as I've already explained. Guys who really like a girl *can't* do that. So if a guy does this, don't let it get to you. Don't let the length of time he takes to reply make you want him more (I know it will, but it's worth a try). Generally, guys play clever text message tactics with girls who are just one of a few they're dating and/or trying to date, and with girls they're just not all that keen on. Not with girls they're desperate to see.

B, the first dater

This is B on first dates – the guy you should watch out for: 'When you've been on a few first dates and know perfectly well that you're not looking for a girlfriend, life becomes easy. You understand how to behave, what to say, what not to say, which stories to tell, how to tell them, where to go and so on. Basically, you develop a reliable strategy, a routine. Sure, it gets boring sometimes but if that happens I would just take a break for a week or two. But I would never forget my strategy.'

Guys on first dates

My view on first dates is that they should not be too complicated. By complicated, I mean difficult to arrange, expensive or elaborate.

Why?

Simple: the more tricky the build-up, the more cash spent on the occasion or the more time wasted putting together a convoluted series of supposedly 'romantic' gestures, the less the occasion becomes about two people meeting up to see how well they get on. Which is, lest we forget, the point of a first date.

So in my view, less is more. Thus, first dates should not be complicated.

The trouble with men and first dates is that when we are in doubt about what to do (basically when we're not sure simply going to a pub or a cafe will impress her) we take the easy option, which is to throw money at the problem. We'll book an expensive restaurant or do something else which is pricy and supposedly impressive.

Men can view first dates a bit like job interviews. Because it's generally up to men to decide where the date happens, we feel like we will be judged by the venue we choose, in the same way at an interview we might be judged at least partly on how smartly dressed we are.

But actually it's not the same thing.

I went through a period of spending quite a lot of money on dates (not loads – I'm not rich, remember). This was fun, but looking back now my priorities were wrong. The evening should be about the two people involved, not the scenery. Expensive restaurants and smart bars are not good venues for entertaining the right kind of girl. After a while I worked out that as long as you're somewhere that basically isn't offensive then you can't really go wrong. And if a girl disagrees and kicks up a fuss, then she can fuss off and find some other mug to date.

I asked a few girls for their views on guys who spend lots of money on dates. There were a few tales of sleazy chaps who think the more cash they throw around, the more of a right they have to expect some kind of sexual reward at the end of the evening. Certainly, for the most part, the girls I spoke to weren't impressed by guys who flash their dough. It's impersonal, presumptive and seemed to lead girls to wonder what he was trying to hide, assuming he wasn't simply setting out to spend and/or flatter his way into her knickers, rather than impressing them. They wanted a guy who had more to impress them with than a credit card. And good for them.

As for going Dutch, I can't do it, especially not on a first date. If a guy has asked a girl out, he should pay for dinner. Full stop. A few dates later, she may want to pay, in which case that's great. And a bit further down the line, when they're fully in a relationship, they might even go Dutch occasionally. But on a first date? No way.

However, that doesn't mean you shouldn't put up a fight. You should *always* put up a fight. Just make sure it's a pretty weak one because the purpose of this little fight is to make him think you're not assuming or expecting that he'll pay. That is not attractive.

Proof that spending money doesn't matter

My first date with Charlotte was on a Sunday afternoon. It was summer so we arranged to meet at the park. That was all. Just a trip to the park. We walked around in the sunshine, sat down for a chat and when the sun started going down went for a pizza. Not complicated, not expensive and not difficult, but it was amazing. Seven months later we were living together.

First dates – the basics

There are many different kinds of first date. For example:

a. Blind date
b. Friend date
c. A date after first meeting but before your first kiss
d. A date after meeting but after your first kiss (and possibly other things too)

Each one raises different questions in a man's mind. They are:

a. Blind date:
    Will I like her?
    Will she like me?
    Will she have sex with me?

b. Friend date
    Will she change her mind about being more than friends?
    Will she have sex with me?

c. A date after first meeting but before your first kiss
    Will she like me?
    Will she have sex with me?

d. A date after meeting but after your first kiss (and possibly other things too)
    Will she like me?
    Will she have sex with me? (add 'again' at the end if appropriate)

All of these can be handled in a similar way. First and foremost, make enjoying the evening your priority. Try as hard as you possibly can not to think beyond that one evening. I know this will be particularly hard if you're in category A or D but you must still try. It is the only way to get the pressure off you.

I'm not suggesting you lower your expectations of your date, simply that in order to have the best time possible you need to set the boundaries in realistic places – i.e. one at the moment you meet and one at the time you go home later.

Don't, for example, start planning out your commute to work from his house when he first tells you where he lives (if you didn't already know). You're setting yourself up for trouble.

I know you're going to do this anyway but I'm still going to say it.

But here's a surprise – men do that too.

Yes, you read correctly. At the first date stage or even before, we also daydream about how a potential relationship might work out. We imagine the girl meeting our friends, our family, weekends together. Obviously we think about what she's going to look like naked as well but one sure-fire way of knowing you really like a girl is if you don't just think about that. And it does happen, far more than we like to admit.

The date and time

Don't be early and don't be on time. Ten minutes late is ideal. When I was single, I used to turn up early for dates so I could get comfortable, know we would have somewhere to sit and relax.

But on my first date with Charlotte I was late. It wasn't my fault because the trains were late, but whatever the cause, my usual rules went out of the window again. I hate being late. Hate it. So I felt terrible and was furious with myself. Especially as she was five minutes early. But it all worked out in the end, which only goes to show that rules are made to be broken. Some are, anyway.

First-date feeding

On a first date you should eat whatever you want. Full stop. You see, men don't mind if you eat in a restaurant. In fact, we like it.

Girls who like their food tend to like other sensory pleasures on offer in life as well. Like sex.

We feel uncomfortable around girls who order tiny amounts of food. Hearing a girl say 'No starter' or 'Just a salad' is not attractive. To guys who are normal (and thus the kind you should be dating), it's plain weird. We don't understand it. So don't do it.

And please, *please*, PLEASE don't be one of those girls who doesn't order chips when she has the chance and then steals them from a guy's plate when his arrive. We would much rather BUY YOU A SECOND LOT OF CHIPS EVEN IF YOU DON'T EAT THEM ALL. Got that?

What to talk about?

I'll keep this bit brief because there really are only two things you should focus on: be yourself and have fun. From his point of view, he'd like you to be good company, which means a bit of flirtatious banter, a bit of fun teasing and being nice to him (for example, you might tell him the bar/pub/greasy spoon cafe you're in was a good choice). The final one will make him happy. The first few will make him like you. And you want him to like you for yourself, right? Of course you do. So be you.

Oh, and don't use that bit about the venue as an excuse to play games with him by pretending to not like a place to see how he reacts. I'm not giving you this information so you can abuse it.

Deal?

Good. I'll carry on.

Guys and their friends

I'm going to step away from first dates now to give you a bit of background on how guys interact with each other. This knowledge will help you understand how to make a guy comfortable with you.

One of my favourite nights out in recent years involved five of my oldest friends and myself. That's five guys I was at school with and had known since I was thirteen – Charlie, Pally, Tom, Ross and Brad. We met in a pub in central London at about 6 p.m., straight after work, and stood in a circle throwing banter at each other and beers down our necks until one by one we lost the ability to stand up. I think I dropped at around 11 p.m. but I can't be sure. The details don't matter.

That banter was triggered by any number of things: daft clothes we've worn, how we talk, girls we've known (and failed to know), nights out when we disgraced ourselves, days out when we disgraced ourselves, the size of our heads (whether small or large – both bases are covered), the size of our bellies (generally growing), height, hair loss – you name it, we pick on it. There's nothing particularly clever or special about this because evenings like ours happen all the time all over the world. Guys are the same wherever they are.

Friends are supposed to be the people who know you best, the ones who see all your faults and accept them. And guys do that, it's just that we also point them out repeatedly and mercilessly for the rest of our lives. From the outside, this can appear mean and possibly boring. But when you're one of the guys inside the magic circle, it's a comfortable, happy place to be, for one simple reason: we only behave that way towards guys we like and know.

Doing the same thing with someone you don't know is bad form. For example, I was in a pub with two school friends and a work colleague of one of them. One of my friends referred to me by an old nickname as is his habit. A few minutes later the work colleague addressed me using the same nickname. My two friends gave him what Paddington Bear would call a hard stare. *They* were allowed to use the nickname because they'd known me for years. But this guy? The guy who only met me an hour before? No way. 'Step back sunshine, you just crossed the line,' was the message. And he got it quickly. He was a guy so he understood.

So, you see, we may appear to be nasty to our friends but we're really as loyal as you can get.

But I still think our friendships are a mystery to girls.

Example: a few years ago I lived with an old university friend, Oli. We got along well. Occasionally he'd get wound up about how messy I was but we never fell out in any major way and we're still great friends now. We were happy living together.

I mention Oli because I remember one evening when his girlfriend Nicola came round and the differences between the two sexes were highlighted brilliantly. Oli and I had got home separately, and we were milling around in the kitchen cooking our food and watching TV. We may have acknowledged each other with a grunt or a nod when a mutually acceptable channel was chosen but beyond that we didn't communicate at all. Nicola couldn't understand this. She was shocked that we were prepared to sit there in silence for a whole evening. 'Why aren't you talking to each other?' she asked.

Oli and I looked at each other and at that moment I'm certain we thought exactly the same thing: I've known him for more than ten years so we've done plenty of talking already, neither of us has anything important or urgent to say, I'm tired and there's something good on TV, so I'm much more interested in watching that than asking how his day went, because if anything unusually good or bad had happened, he'd have told me by now.

In a nutshell, we had nothing to say so we said nothing. And we were both perfectly happy. I think Nicola was gradually learning that, unlike female friendships, male ones aren't based on knowing the minutiae of each other's lives.

Can girls spend evenings like that? Judging from what I've seen and heard over the years, no, they can't.

The point is, I understand how the interaction between male friends can appear bizarre. But it's not strange at all, really. We tease each other because it's fun and it means we know our friends well enough to be confident enough in their loyalty to take the banter as well as give it. And we don't feel the need to fill silences because, well, we quite like silence sometimes. And that's it. We're not aliens.

Two quotes about friendship

I love random quotes about different subjects. Read these two quotes about friendship from men and you should understand:

'If you press me to say why I loved him, I can say no more than it was because he was he, and I was I.' **Michel de Montaigne**

'A true friend stabs you in the front.' **Oscar Wilde**

One final thought on male friendships

A few years ago I read an article by an American lesbian writer who went undercover as a man for a few months as research for a book about guys. She did some weights, cut her hair short, had some fake facial hair put on, strapped down her breasts and wore suits. This woman was expecting nothing more than to confirm her preconceptions about what guys are like when women aren't around – namely lecherous, rude, unpleasant and nowhere near as nice as ladies.

But it didn't quite turn out like that. Men surprised her. For a start, the guys she met – normal, working-class Americans – were completely honest with each other about clothes. Apparently (and I know this is true) if a girl turns up to meet her friends wearing a new top, her friends will very often tell her it looks great and the colour really suits her, no matter how offensive they find the garment and no matter how terrible they think she looks in it. This is obviously lying. Guys, however, behave differently.

Imagine the evening I described earlier, the one where the six of us stood in a circle drinking beer for a few hours. If one of us had rocked up in some kind of outlandish clobber – a garish new shirt or some bravely flamboyant shoes – which any one of the rest of the group disapproved of or even just noticed as new or out of the ordinary, someone would immediately point at the new garment and say something like, 'What the hell is that?' Inevitably, much of the next hour would be spent talking about what a terrible decision it was to spend money on such a thing. And the kicker is that the guy who made the fashion 'error' wouldn't mind. In fact he'd probably wear the same thing again next time the guys met up.

The lesbian American writer found this fascinating and quite endearing. She liked men's honesty in comparison to women's passive/aggressive pseudo-approval.

She also – and this was the bit she was really surprised by – saw the guys being very nice about their wives and girlfriends. Loyal, loving, appreciative and complimentary, in fact. And then they were nice to each other, too. Each was genuinely concerned about how the others were doing in their lives and – oh, the shock – they even talked about their *feelings*.

By the end of her undercover sting, she liked men far more than she had ever expected.

So there you have it. A lesbian liked men when there were no women around, which means you should too.

Now, back to first dates.

First-date protocols

So, to recap: how do you arrange a first date? Let the guy do it. Why? Because guys like to feel like they're pursuing something of value and they need to feel like they're making an effort (remember the roadkill moose). And from what I've learned over the years, girls like to feel like they're being wooed anyway, so letting the guy do the arranging works for everyone.

How do you arrive at a first date? With a smile.

When do you arrive? Aim to be between five and ten minutes late.

What should you talk about on a first date? Anything but your exes.

What should you eat? Whatever you want.

How much should you drink? Enough to have fun but not enough to get carried away.

How should you end a first date? That depends entirely on how it went but the most sensible option is to go home separately. However, as we all know, that doesn't always happen, however good your intentions are.

An unsuccessful first date

On a first date, it is perfectly natural to ask the person you're with lots of questions. I understand this. Of course I do. I know girls are naturally inquisitive creatures and I'm very happy with that. In fact I quite like being asked questions on a date because it shows that the person doing the asking is interested in me.

But there are limits to how nosy a girl should be. Obvious potential minefield topics include how you broke up with your ex or how many people you've slept with. These are best left unexplored until you know each other better. Or even not at all.

There are other subjects that can ruin an evening despite appearing harmless at first, as I found out on one first date. I was out for a few drinks with a girl called Sam who I met in a bar after a friend of mine started chatting up a friend of hers. From the start of the evening she was asking me a lot of questions. She went through some fairly innocuous ones (favourite food, where I'm from, political allegiance, etc.) that were easy to answer before blindsiding me with: 'When did you last cry?'

Now, I'm a modern man and not averse to showing my emotions but I thought this was odd because I hardly knew the girl. But I went with the flow and thought of the two times I'd cried in recent memory. The one further back, and so not the honest answer to Sam's question, was when Herbie, our beloved family dog, was put to sleep while I held him in my arms. And oh, did I cry then.

Despite the obvious benefits of telling this story (surely she'd have been overcome with desire for me after I revealed my sensitive side), I told Sam the truth, namely that it was at a football match, two weekends previously, when Cambridge United, the football team I've supported since I was knee-high to a goalkeeper, lost an indescribably important game to Exeter City (I won't go into the details – I know you're not interested). Being a lifelong Cambridge fan this game meant a great deal to me. To Sam, however, it meant nothing.

Actually, make that less than nothing. Because after I answered her question she looked at me for a second before bursting out laughing.

'You're so sad,' she said, when the giggles faded. 'That's pathetic!' At first I thought she was joking but she added: 'Are you serious? It's only Cambridge United.'

Only Cambridge United? What the hell was she thinking? The emotional wounds I suffered from that match were still too raw for me to be able to formulate a polite response so I stayed quiet. I had a long swig of beer and tried to calm down. It didn't work and the date went downhill fast after that. In fact, I was on my way home alone about half an hour later having decided I was not going to see her again.

I know perfectly well that by any rational judgement it's ridiculous to cry about football, but why should she react like that? Sam obviously wanted me to be a sensitive new-age man in touch with my emotions and so on, which is absolutely fine. But she has no right to then complain if I get emotional about something of which she doesn't approve. If I'm not ashamed of shedding tears for my football team, then Sam shouldn't be either. She can't have it both ways.

If a girl doesn't understand football (I know some do, like my little sister, for example), and by 'football' I mean the emotional commitment which goes with supporting a team as well as the offside rule, she should still accept it. That's all, just accept it.

Don't judge, just accept.

Don't criticise, just accept.

Don't question, just accept.

And you're allowed to mock occasionally but only on condition that you do the required accepting first.

Got that? Good. I'll move on again.

Online dating

This is going to be a short section because I haven't done much of it. Any, in fact. But my friends have and consequently I think I've got it cracked.

Apart from not knowing what a guy looks like, there is, I believe, only one major difference between meeting a guy online and in real life: the fact that online you communicate with strangers with no context whatsoever.

What exactly does that mean?

Well, if you meet a guy in a bar, you will assume certain things about him, even if you don't realise you're doing it. Your subconscious will have taken note of his height, whether or not he's attractive, if he looks healthy, how he approached you (if he approached you), his clothes, his age, what his friends are like (if he's with any) and even where you are. You will make assumptions about him without even realising it and these assumptions will lead you to like or not like him. He might even be a friend of a friend. Your subconscious will make calculations extremely quickly, working out in less than a blink of your eye what kind of person he's likely to be on the basis of all the available evidence, which is much more than you consciously realise. All you know about this process is your gut instinct telling you either 'Ooh, he's nice' or 'Get that weirdo away from me' almost instantly.

Online, there's none of that, so every bit of information given or received takes on a disproportionately large importance because that is literally *all* you know about the person you're in touch with. And so these things can be taken out of context.

This is something my friend Greg completely failed to realise. Greg is seriously intelligent. I mean he has a brain the size of Russia. Greg is a very, very clever man. He's also funny and interesting. But he is single, which is how he came to be on an internet dating site talking to a girl about a book they both liked, *On Chesil Beach* by Ian McEwan (a book about a newly married couple's disastrous attempts at sex on their honeymoon). As their literary discourse continued, Greg said he thought the book was really about child abuse and that the main female character reacted to her husband as she did because of some traumatic experience in her youth – i.e. she was abused. Now, I happen to agree with Greg and we talked about this at some length while he was telling me his online dating story.

It was OK for him to talk to me about this because Greg knows me and I know Greg. This girl on the dating site, however, had never even seen Greg in the flesh and knew nothing about him. Except that he reads books about child abuse.

Which is not ideal in a potential dating scenario.

Their conversation didn't last long after that. Poor Greg, I thought. He didn't even get as far as a first date. Lesson learned though: don't mention child abuse when you're trying to chat up a girl. Obvious to some people, you'd think. But not Greg, despite his mammoth IQ. Strange.

When first dates go bad (has to be said in dramatic US TV voiceover style)

Here's another of my first-date stories. This one is useful because it shows how girls should not behave if they want to have a good time and be liked, because for a first date to be a success, it has to be fun. Everyone knows that, don't they?

No, they don't. And here's how I found out.

When winter is particularly cold, February is a miserable month. And so in an effort to banish the winter blues, I started reading a brilliant book about all the good things in life. It was called *It Is Just You, Everything's Not Shit* and was full of simple things that make you happy, ranging from breakfast in bed to Bagpuss and the beauty of white clouds in a blue sky. I'm a glass-half-full person and I love things like this.

The book put me in a good mood for a winter date with a girl I had met just before Christmas. We met at a party and she seemed fun.

But I discovered she was also a little bit grumpy.

As soon as she sat down, she sighed and started unloading her stresses on me. On and on she went and after hearing her complain about the cold weather for the fiftieth time I mentioned this book to try to lighten the atmosphere. I started telling her about clouds and how appreciating simple things like that can cheer you up.

'But they're only clouds,' she said, looking at me like I was a simpleton.

'I know that,' I replied patiently. 'But the point is that even though they are just clouds, they're beautiful and all you have to do to enjoy them is look up at the sky. There's no effort involved and it's free.'

She looked at me blankly.

'I don't get it. They're just clouds. What's so special about them?'

If I need to explain, you'll never understand, I thought, and at this point I was tempted to get the bill before she dragged me down with her.

But I was hungry and we hadn't got on to the main course yet so I ploughed on, trying my hardest to perk up the evening. I got nowhere.

She moaned about everything: work (too many hours, not enough salary), family (too demanding of her time, not giving enough of their own) and friends (too distant when she wants them, too needy when they want her – there's a pattern emerging here). By 10 p.m. I had to get out.

I knew that if I drank much more I'd start being gratuitously offensive so I mumbled something about a breakfast meeting the following morning, an obvious lie that I'm sure she saw through, and paid the bill (I'd asked her out, remember, so it was my responsibility). Outside, I got her a taxi and legged it in the opposite direction.

All I could think was that I'd wasted a night out. This girl was so far off my wavelength it was ridiculous. I'm hardly a hippy tree-hugger but if you can't appreciate the simple beauty of the world around you then in my eyes you've got the wrong approach to life.

But it seems bad moods are infectious. I was grumpy all the way home. It was too bloody dark to see any clouds at all.

A rubbish, depressing first date.

Lesson: be positive on first dates.

My first blind date

About two months after I broke up with Girlfriend Y, a friend of mine asked if I wanted to go on a blind date. My first reaction was absolutely not. I'd never been on a blind date before and thought they sounded hellish. And besides, at the time I was happy and enjoying my still fairly new freedom, dating girls here and there, dipping my toe in the shallow end of the dating pool, if you like.

The one thing I wasn't looking for was a girlfriend, as Giles's words about being single for at least a year were still fresh in my mind.

So when my friend said she wanted me to go on this blind date with her 'really nice' friend, I gave an honest reaction.

'It's not a good idea,' I said. 'I don't want to go on a blind date and anyway, I don't want a girlfriend because I haven't been single for long enough so there's no point in me meeting her. I don't want any kind of commitment. You don't want to send me on a date with your friend. At the moment I'm not a good bet.'

'Whatever,' she said, hardly listening to me. 'You two will have fun.'

'That's the problem,' I protested. 'All I want is to have fun. I don't want anything serious. Girls shouldn't be sent on blind dates with guys in that state of mind.'

But she persisted.

'She's only just broken up with someone too so you're in the same boat. They were together for ten years and she doesn't want a boyfriend.'

'What?' I said. 'That just means she's vulnerable. What kind of friend are you?'

'Shut up. You're going to see her.'

I made my friend promise to repeat every word of this conversation to my blind date before she agreed to go on that blind date with me. My conscience wouldn't let me do it any other way. Apparently this wasn't a problem, so I was put in touch with her friend and we arranged to meet.

A quick tangent before the date story

I arrived twenty minutes early for the blind date. I went into the pub, got myself a beer and sat down at a table with that day's London *Evening Standard*. Very quickly I found myself feeling extremely happy. I mean, how often do men go to the pub on their own for a pint and a quiet read of a newspaper or a book? Never. And that's a crying shame because it is a wonderful way to pass a bit of time.

I found myself hoping Blind-Date Girl would be late.

Unfortunately she wasn't.

Back to the date story

As soon as she arrived I did the first thing I could think of – legged it to the bar to buy her a drink. Under the cunning disguise of good manners (getting the first round in), I ran away and hid.

And I thought about whether or not I was disappointed with what I saw.

Don't pretend to be surprised at that. Or disappointed in me. Of course that was the first thing I thought about. As soon as a blind date becomes non-blind, the first thing a guy notices is what she looks like. I would be very surprised if the same isn't true for girls, by the way.

So what did I think?

What girls mean when they say 'pretty'

Over the years, whether it was in a conversation about me being set up or not, I've noticed that girls always overestimate how attractive their friends are. Girls call another girl 'pretty' if she simply has no outstanding physical flaws. Or 'really pretty' if she sits at what men think of as the lowest end of the attractiveness scale. When assessing other girls, they seem to be unable to gauge how attractive she is. Attractive being different to pretty.

This girl was attractive, but tall and slender, which we've already established was not my usual physical type. And no, that doesn't mean I liked short, fat girls, just that I prefer girls with curves. Got that?

Anyway, we started talking and things were, to be honest, a

little bit awkward. A few drinks made things better. Not great, but definitely better. At the end of the night we kissed goodbye (thank you, alcohol) and went our separate ways.

But the night wasn't over because at 1 a.m. I got a message from her saying, 'I'm so turned on I can't go to sleep.'

My friend was right, I thought. Blind-Date Girl really did just want a bit of fun. There's no way I'd have had a message like this if she wanted anything serious, especially after she'd been briefed about me before we went.

So how did our bit of fun turn out?

It didn't.

The blow-out

I actually never saw her again because as of two days later she completely blanked me. I didn't understand why until our mutual friend told me some months later that the day after the blind date, an old friend of Blind-Date Girl declared his undying love to her. She declared hers back and that was it, they've been together ever since. And I'm pleased about that – I like people ending up happy.

But it did make me wonder if my friend was right when she said Blind-Date Girl was only up for something casual. Maybe she'd secretly fancied this guy for years and unless it was him she was involved with, she wouldn't want anything serious. Who knows?

I certainly don't – she never spoke to me again!

Finally, here are my top twenty-five date tips:

1. Don't be tired, hungover or grumpy. You want to have fun and he wants to have fun.
2. Feel free to suggest a venue – he *should* do this, but it's not a golden rule and if he isn't hugely confident he might appreciate the suggestion. The way to do it is say something like, 'I'd love to try this new place . . .' or 'Do you know xx bar/restaurant? I love it there . . .' Your enthusiasm will help him relax because he won't worry about the venue any more and you'll be able to relax knowing you're going somewhere you like.
3. Before you go on your date, imagine yourself having a good time with him and feeling confident and happy. Sportsmen do something similar before big games – they visualise themselves doing great things and winning to boost their confidence. It's a useful trick if you're the nervous type and also works for job interviews etc.
4. Make an effort to look good. That includes natural-looking make-up. Too much isn't good.
5. Dress well but make sure you wear something you are comfortable in. Really low-cut tops aren't a great idea. You want him to look at your face, not your boobs. And if he likes you, the chances are he won't remember what you wore on your first date anyway (sorry, but that's the truth), so it won't matter anyway.
6. Wear a little bit of perfume. Enough to smell tantalisingly good but not so much he can't breathe properly.
7. Your ideal arrival window is between bang on time and

five to ten minutes late but don't worry if you're early or late. Unless you're ridiculously late (i.e. half an hour or more), it won't make or break your date.

8. Don't chew gum. You're not an American teenager.

9. When you see him, relax and smile. Look happy and welcoming.

10. 'Hello' should be a kiss on the cheek. The start of a date is too early for a hug. Let him initiate this.

11. If you like him, make eye contact early in the date. This establishes the connection between the two of you and lays the foundations for some flirtation.

12. If you really like him, make the eye contact linger.

13. If you get nervous at any stage, focus on breathing slowly and deeply. This is guaranteed to calm you down. Just make sure you're subtle – you don't want to look like you're having an asthma attack.

14. Ask questions but not too many (it's not an interrogation) and make them on subjects you think he'll be happy talking about. Make him relaxed and comfortable and you'll see the best of him as your date goes on.

15. Listen to what he says. You like to be listened to, right? Do the same for him.

16. Don't be afraid to tease him. I don't mean sexually (save that for later dates). I mean gently mocking him. Men think this is fun and we like girls who do this to us. That said, subjects to steer clear of include his hair (if he's losing it), his weight (if he's gaining it), his bank balance (unless he does it first) and his mother (*always* off limits).

17. Be positive and happy about life. You don't have to insist everything in your world is perfect (no one's life is like

that) but don't spend your whole time moaning about work, your commute, the weather, etc. etc.

18. Don't brag about how amazing you are or be too aggressive. It's a date not a competition.

19. Pre-date Dutch courage is not a good idea. In general guys can drink more than girls, so if you have already had a head start you may find yourself in trouble further down the line. Which leads us to . . .

20. Don't drink too much on the date. The reasons for this are obvious.

21. Eat. And not just because of the previous tip. Eating is good. Not eating is bad, both for your health and for the impression you're trying to make. Girls who don't eat aren't sexy.

22. Don't talk about your exes or ask about his. On the first date you're starting to build a fire of romance between the two of you and at this moment – when the sparks are beginning to appear – talking about exes will destroy that spark like a bucket of cold water.

23. Do kiss him goodbye if you like him and want to. But if you like him, don't go any further. Do not go home with him. I repeat: IF YOU LIKE THE GUY DO NOT GO HOME WITH HIM AFTER YOUR FIRST DATE.

24. Leave him wanting more. If it's late and you're having a great time, don't be afraid to cut things off then and there. It's time to go home no matter how much fun you're having and if you want to see him again, leaving him wanting more increases the chances of him calling you.

25. Don't think about the second date until you get home from the first one. Follow my tips and you'll have the

best possible chance of having a second one. Worrying about it while you're on the first will make you tense and stop you enjoying yourself, thus you won't appear in your best light.

NOTE:
Most of these tips can be used just as easily by guys as girls.

Chapter Five

Making Him Call You

- How to know if he's interested or not
- Why men call or don't call
- If he's wavering, how to make up his mind for him
- When to call or text back and what to say

Have you ever met a single guy who says about a single girl: 'I didn't like her much at first but eventually she won me over'?

No, you haven't (if either person is not single they don't count).

That is because if a guy doesn't fancy a girl as soon as he meets her, it's extremely unlikely that he's ever going to change his mind. Guys, you see, work differently to girls. First impressions last much longer for us and if we don't have that immediate buzz when we see or meet a girl for the first time, then the chances are it's never going to happen. It might do, of course, but the percentage chance is so tiny that for your purposes that chance is zero. So remember this: if a guy doesn't fancy a girl as soon as he meets her, he won't change his mind.

Linked to that point is my generalised theory that guys become extremely keen on girls far more quickly than girls do with men. A guy can really fall for a girl in a few days or weeks whereas I don't think girls really fall for guys for a few months. They can be infatuated, yes. But really falling? That takes longer, maybe even months. Guys definitely do it quicker, even if they don't show it.

The point is this: while *you* may look at a guy and think he might not make your heart flutter right now but he definitely has the potential to grow on you, guys do not think like that. If a girl doesn't fire us up from day one, we're not interested. But if a girl does fire us up, we want to be near her as much as possible as soon as possible.

When I met Charlotte, I couldn't stop thinking about her, I couldn't wait to see her again and I hated saying goodbye at the end of our dates because if we didn't already have another meeting arranged, I'd worry that I might not see her again. I know that sounds wildly melodramatic but it's an honest description of how I felt. I fell for her very hard in a matter of hours.

That's how guys are when they really like someone.

Contact and communication

One of the consequences of writing my dating column was that people started asking my advice about their own dating lives. In the early days of the column I didn't feel I had much to offer in the way of expertise so shied away from trying to help. But as the months went on, I realised I was accumulating enough of the right kind of wisdom to actually be able to offer them something useful because I was thinking and analysing far more than I ever had.

And there was one question which girls asked me more often than any other. This question would be expressed in different ways, but it always boiled down to the same thing: 'Why hasn't he called me?' Trying to answer it satisfactorily seemed, at first, highly complicated because I needed to pick my way through the psychology of not only the girl asking the question but also the guy involved. So I would ask questions back about her and him, how they met, how many times they'd been out, what he said and so on.

Worst of all, I joined in on the analysis of texts they'd sent each other before he went quiet on her (these conversations were virtually always prompted by the guy going quiet on the girl). The endless rounds of 'What do you think this means?' and 'Why did he say this?' and 'Should I have said that differently?' and 'What shall I say back to him?', where every possible interpretation of the dialogue is explored. I mean *every* possible interpretation – the nuances of words, the placement of commas, the time of day and even his tone.

After each of these discussions, I thought and thought and thought about the best advice I could give. Every situation is different, I believed, and so requires different advice, which I dutifully gave.

It was hard work but I felt I was doing the right thing by these girls. But then, after five or six girls had been blessed with the benefits of my carefully considered advice, I realised that while every situation might look different at first glance, when you dig just a little deeper, they're all the same. I noticed this when I realised the advice I'd given was identical every time.

After that the conversations became much, much shorter. They went like this:

Girl: 'There's this guy and I haven't heard from him and I

want to text him or call him but I don't know what to say because I don't know what he thinks.'

Me: 'Don't say anything. Don't text and don't call. Move on.'

Girl: 'What? But how will I know if he likes me?'

Me: 'You know already because he hasn't been in touch. If he really liked you he would want to see you and if he wanted to see you he'd have got in touch. Move on and find someone who likes you enough to call you.'

Girl: 'But—'

Me: 'Goodbye.'

I do care, honest

I might come across a bit harsh there but the point I tried to make was that you can analyse and analyse what is or isn't or might or might not be going on in a man's mind as much as you want (which will either be a lot or next to nothing, if my experience is anything to go by) but you will never get beyond guesswork. Nothing will be certain.

The one single thing you can know for sure when a guy hasn't called you is that *he hasn't called you*.

And what does that mean?

Well, if he hasn't called you, he can't be all that interested, can he? I mean, do you *not call* people you like? Whether that's friends or potential boyfriends, would you demonstrate your affection for them by not being in contact? By not texting, calling, emailing, Tweeting, Facebooking or instant messaging for weeks on end? Well, would you? Think about that for a second.

No. Of course you bloody wouldn't.

Guys are actually the same as girls in that way (once we've left primary school, anyway). We like to communicate with and even see (shock, horror) people we're fond of, too. Especially girls.

So here's what to say to a guy who isn't calling you: nothing.

I don't mean a silent phone call (you're not a stalker), I simply mean that if he's not making the effort then you shouldn't have to.

What does it say if you text a guy who hasn't called you?

Rightly or wrongly, it's a man's job to make the running, not yours. Blame genetics, blame twenty-first-century gender politics, blame the tyranny of men, blame the feminist movement of the 1960s, blame whoever or whatever you want. I don't mind. I'm only interested in what's actually happening today between single or dating adults, not the social anthropology behind it all, fascinating though I'm sure it is.

Evolutionary science apart, the upshot is that guys expect, consciously or not, to be the one making the running with girls. Like the moose hunter in Chapter One, we value things we have to work for, and if you call or text a guy you haven't heard from, you make it easy for him. Too easy. Because we don't value things we get easily. In fact, you'd be a roadkill moose. On a plate.

You want a guy who likes you

I'm just guessing here but I don't think you want to date a guy who isn't almost uncontrollably drawn to you from the moment you meet.

Am I right?

Of course I am.

You shouldn't have to text him or call him to try to remind him that he likes you or get him interested enough to want to see you. He shouldn't need reminders that you exist and are lovely.

If you need to remind him, it's wrong.

So keep your dignity intact, stop pining and remember that if he stops calling after a couple of dates or doesn't call at all after taking your number, it's only your confidence and pride that have been hurt. Emotions – the place where you can really get hurt – don't kick in with a new guy until much later.

Why men don't call

There are many reasons why men don't call. Busy with work, no free nights to see you, going on holiday, doctor's appointments, whatever. There are loads.

But they really all boil down to the same thing. As the book (and film) famously said of guys who are a bit flaky: he's just not that into you. And 99% of the time that is absolutely bang on the money.

Actually, he might be into you (sorry)

Remember I talked about how every rule I give you about the best way to handle men has an exception, that one in one hundred that doesn't follow the pattern? Well, there are exceptions to this one, too. On behalf of the male species, I'm ashamed to admit there are men out there who will not call girls they like. Today, when you can communicate with a girl by any number of ways that are less intimidating than phoning (text, email, Facebook, etc.), there really is no excuse for this behaviour. But these guys do exist.

I'm only telling you this because I promised to be completely honest.

So you know these guys exist. What should you do about it?

Nothing. There it is again – *doing nothing is often the right thing to do.*

How can you tell if the guy you like is one of them?

If he doesn't call, he might be one of these very shy men. The chances are miniscule, but he might be. But the overwhelming probability is that he's not one of these guys and he simply isn't that interested in calling you. You have to assume he's the rule, not the exception.

And even if he is the exception, do you really want to date a guy who hasn't got the balls to call you? No, I didn't think so. A *bit* shy, nervous or awkward is fine. But not someone who won't even call you.

Why men call sometimes, when things are great, but then go quiet...

Let's say you've dated a guy a handful of times, up to seven or eight. When you're with him things are great, intense, fun and passionate. But when you're not with him – between dates – there's nothing. This means one of two things: either he's happily enjoying the early stages of dating you and expecting things will blossom into something more serious, or he just wants a fun night with you every now and then, and when you're not together he's not thinking about you because he's not that bothered in the longer term.

How can you tell which is which? You can't be certain until his behaviour proves it. That is to say at some stage he will either vanish completely or start hanging out with you on Sunday evenings and ask you to meet his parents. What to do until then? Trust your instincts and be careful because if I was being super cautious, I'd say the odds are that the 'occasional' guy won't turn into the 'forever' guy. He might, but it's not likely.

Why men don't call at all

He's not interested in you.

Why men don't call for a few days/weeks

He's seeing someone else and is waiting to see how that pans out before he goes out with you. Or he's busy and is going to wait until he gets bored before he calls you.

Neither seem like brilliant prospects, do they?

Can your badly worded texts mess it up?

If he likes you (and by 'like' I mean wants to see you again and/or get you into bed), then it is just about impossible for you to mess things up with any dodgy texts or emails. If you send a message you think might or might not have sent out the wrong signals, it doesn't matter. If he likes you he likes you and if he doesn't, he doesn't. Your slightly ambiguous text will make no difference whatsoever. The decision has already been made. In fact, if you send him a slightly clumsy and embarrassing message that will probably make him like you even more because he'll know you like him and are a little bit kooky. We like that.

What this means, I'm sorry to say, is that the vast majority of those endless 'Did I say the right thing?'/'Is he going to call me?'/'Does he like me?' conversations are a waste of time. I'm not saying you girls should stop them or are wrong for enjoying them, just that they don't really achieve much in relation to the guy you're talking about.

Example – me again

When I met Charlotte, I knew straight away that I wanted to see her again. I took her number on a Sunday and on the Monday I texted to arrange a date for that week. Unfortunately there were diary clashes all week so we arranged to meet on the following Sunday. This was unusual for me – I hadn't had a Sunday afternoon date before. But I wanted to see her as soon as possible so thought why not?

The first point is that I got in touch with her pretty well straight away because I liked her a lot. In fact, I couldn't stop thinking about her. That meant I wanted to be with her again as soon as possible. All the conventions about playing it cool, leaving it a couple of days and so on went out of the window. This was partly because I wanted the reassurance I was going to see her again as soon as possible and also because I trusted my instincts which told me she'd prefer for me to get in touch sooner rather than later, and wasn't interested in playing any games on that score.

With the date arranged, I then faced another problem: I had six days to wait.

Momentum – how important is it?

I really wanted to be in touch with Charlotte (I was thinking about her all the time, remember), but I didn't know her well enough to have general chit-chat over the days leading up to our first date. I held out until Thursday, when I texted to check we were still on for the Sunday. I know – there were still three days left which meant it was a pretty lame excuse, but I couldn't think of anything else to say. What else could I ask her? 'How are you?' Even lamer. 'What have you been up to?' Worse.

So all I was left with was: 'Are you still on for Sunday?' But I wanted to be in contact with Charlotte and I hoped she wanted to be in touch with me. In fact, I made a decision to take a risk. I decided that if Charlotte was the kind of girl I thought and hoped she was, she would want to be in touch with me too.

When I like someone – and I knew there was something special between us before we'd even spoken so yes, I liked her – I am not very good at playing it by the book. And I don't want to play it by the book either. I want to be able to be absolutely true to myself. I don't want to be governed by *The Rules* or moves and tricks I've learned in the past as effective ways to make a girl keen on you. I wanted it to be natural, to feel unique and special. And with Charlotte, it did.

What about Charlotte? What did she do?

Charlotte didn't text me in that week leading up to the date until I texted her on that Thursday. And I spent the whole week thinking about her and couldn't wait for the Sunday to come.

Let me repeat that: Charlotte didn't do anything proactive all week, other than reply to my messages. She didn't instigate contact at all. The result was me spending the week thinking about her and wondering if she was thinking about me too (OK, hoping she was thinking about me too). By the end of the week, I couldn't wait to see her. And she'd done nothing. Nothing at all.

See?

So what happened?

She was still on for Sunday and that first date worked out very, very well.

I'm telling this story to make the point that when a guy likes a girl, he wants to be in touch with her. He wants to know she's thinking about him and he wants to know he's going to see her again, like I was with Charlotte. We want to be sure we are doing everything we can to make what we want happen.

So the general rule is this: *if a guy doesn't contact a girl, he doesn't want to see her.*

But that doesn't always mean he doesn't *like* her. Or at least he thinks he likes her. OK, that doesn't make sense. Let me use an example.

My non-contact story

I've already told you about how important timing is in the cycle of a single guy's life but I have another example that is useful here.

In the brief period between breaking up with Girlfriend X and meeting Girlfriend Y, I met a girl called Caroline who was very nice.

'Very nice' – that doesn't sound great, does it? If you're reading between the lines, I bet you're not imagining fireworks going off between us.

We met at a mutual friend's party. I took her number and we went out three or four times but things didn't get serious. She was, as I said, a very nice girl. By very nice, I mean she was pretty, friendly, clever, fun and all those good things. She was what some guys call 'girlfriend material'.

But there was a problem. And that problem was me.

I'd broken up with Girlfriend X about three months previously and thus was in no state whatsoever to get into anything serious. So when we'd been out three or four times and things looked like they were about to step up a level between us, I stopped calling her. I was young and cowardly and instead of phoning up and saying, 'I'm really sorry but I'm only recently out of a relationship and while I think you're great, I can't do this right now,' I just disappeared. I'm not proud of myself at all.

The points

There are two points to make after telling this story. OK, make that three, the third one being that it was not nice of me to treat her like this. I know that.

Anyway, back to my points.

Point 1: I didn't stop calling her because I wasn't interested. At the time, I was interested in her but I knew I was in the wrong place mentally to be part of the kind of relationship which was clearly about to develop, so I backed off (in a pathetic, childish way).

Point 2: Looking back on all this, I see things differently now. While at the time I *thought* I was genuinely interested in Caroline, I now know I wasn't. Because if I had been, there's no way I'd have let her get away back then. I'd have made her mine before someone else did.

So here's the point: if a guy tells you he's not interested

in taking things further with you because the timing is wrong for him, as it was for me and Caroline, he *believes* he is telling you the truth even though he isn't. So that means you shouldn't be harsh on him because, I repeat, he sincerely believes he's being honest with you. The fact he doesn't know how he really feels is not a reason to judge him harshly. In fact, it only goes to give extra weight to the words above: *if a guy doesn't contact a girl, he doesn't want to see her.* Remember those words.

Point 3: I was an idiot. I should have told her how I (believed) I felt.

Was I right about Caroline?

Once a guy has stopped dating a girl due to 'bad timing', it's very, very rare that the two people involved ever get together properly at some point in the future. Most pairs (note – I didn't say couples) who have experienced a situation like that continue to stay apart.

I'll try to think of some that have ended up together at a later date.

Any, in fact.

Give me a minute.

No, nothing yet.

Still nothing.

OK, I give up, I can't think of any.

And what does that tell us? It tells us that my view in hindsight regarding my feelings about Caroline (that I wasn't interested enough) was right. And given that I can't think of any examples of any similar situations that turned out differently, well, you get the picture, don't you?

Timing, schmiming.

MEN SENSE:

1. If he hasn't called after a date, assume he's not interested.
2. If he takes more than two or three days to call, assume he's not interested.
3. When you text him back, leave it an hour at first (if you like him) and then just a bit longer than he does every time after that.
4. You can be inactive and proactive at the same time – leaving the ball in his court is good.
5. Worrying about sending a bad text is a waste of time. If he likes you it won't matter. Really.

Chapter Six

First Sex with a New Guy

- Why the first one doesn't matter
- Don't be too naughty too soon
- Why men's egos need to be stroked too
- How to stroke that ego

Despite this chapter's suggestive title, I'm not going to get explicit and start writing about sex in graphic detail.

Why the modesty? Well, it's not because I'm trying to protect my reputation in the eyes of my mother and sisters. Nor am I behaving like the stereotypical repressed Englishman, who is easily embarrassed when talking about the minutiae of sexual activities (in reality that is me to a T but right now that's irrelevant).

No, the reason I'm going to avoid bringing up details when talking about sex is this: for men, sex is not about details.

What *is* sex about for men?

When a man is single, sex satisfies his basic urges and makes him feel less lonely and insecure about whether or not girls find him attractive (which is why single men are so sex-obsessed when they've been drinking: all those urges and insecurities are magnified and transformed into rampant horniness).

And when a man is in a relationship sex is about him and his girlfriend loving each other – the affirmation and celebration of a happy, loving and fulfilling coupling between two people.

Not being a girl, I might well be wrong when I say this, but I suspect the female view on sex isn't hugely different. Including the bit about alcohol-enhanced horniness.

But that is not to say men and women are the same in every way.

The scene from *Friends*

Cast your mind back a few years to Ross and Rachel's first kiss. To recap, they kiss passionately after arguing at Central Perk. Ross goes to see Joey and Chandler while, in the flat across the hall, Rachel is talking to Phoebe and Monica.

Over a bottle of wine and with much excitement, Rachel recounts every detail of how Ross kissed her, starting with where he put his hands. 'First, they started out on my waist, and then they slid up, and then they were in my hair...' Phoebe and Monica can barely speak because they're so absorbed in the story. The only sounds they make are little gasps and squeals.

Then cut to the guys, who are standing over the foosball

table, eating pizza. Ross says, 'And er . . . and then I kissed her.'

'Tongues?' asks Joey.

'Yeah,' says Ross.

'Cool,' says Joey, and they all nod and carry on eating their pizza. And that's it – conversation over.

Everyone loved *Friends*. It was funny, unthreatening, the characters were immensely likeable and best of all the storylines – young adults falling in and out of love while trying to make their way in the world – felt true to anyone who was either at that stage of their lives, had been through it or even those who were looking forward to being grown-up enough to live in a flat with a chicken and a duck and two gorgeous girls across the hall (I was and it never happened – another shattered dream).

And never in the whole show (236 episodes over ten series from 1994 to 2004 – I checked) was a moment truer to real life than the one I just described. That conversation between Ross and Chandler and Joey is one all men have, not just fictitious American ones who live in luxurious apartments they clearly wouldn't be able to afford in the real world.

What that means is that when it comes to talking about girls who mean something to us in the way Rachel meant something to Ross, we don't talk about the details. Quite simply, they are sacred, to be kept between us and the lady (for this girl really is a lady). It is a Man Rule. Joey and Chandler knew this and Ross knew Joey and Chandler knew this. And so their conversation was short but effective – in a manly way. All the information Ross's friends needed (that is, they kissed and Ross was happy about it) was imparted.

And so, reassured that their friend was successfully wooing a girl he loved, Joey and Chandler could relax and go back to eating pizza. We men like feeling that way.

Humfrey Hunter

The secret to good sex

Someone – I can't remember who, which is a shame – once told me that for a couple to have guaranteed good sex every time they need only two things. The couple doesn't need anything else, just these two things.

When I heard this I started wondering what on earth those things could be. What secrets could exist out there that I'd never even heard of and that were so amazing they would guarantee great sex every time?

Every time?

Yes indeed, this person told me, every time.

Wow. They must be some special secrets.

But when the answer came, I was a little disappointed because all I got were two words. Only eight syllables. Nine if you can be bothered to count the 'and' between them.

So what were the words?

After much fanfare and dramatic tension, they were revealed to me as these: affection and enthusiasm.

And that's it. Ho hum. (That's me being underwhelmed, by the way.)

When I first heard these words I wasn't convinced that they really were the silver bullet of sexual fulfilment. I was young(ish) at the time and, more importantly, single, so sex with someone I loved was not a fresh memory. But once I thought about it a bit longer and got a bit older and became more experienced in the ways of both the heart and the bedroom, I realised that whoever it was who gave me that golden nugget was absolutely right.

Do this with me: imagine you are with someone you genuinely

like and respect as a person, who you feel you connect with, who you want to get to know better, whose emails, phone calls or texts are the highlight of your day, who makes you feel content and calm *and* who you also find extremely physically attractive. So attractive you want to be alone and naked with them *right now*.

Then imagine the person feels exactly the same about you. Enjoy that for a moment or two.

Now imagine having sex with them.

Isn't that nice?

Thus if you have affection and enthusiasm between two people, everything else sexual should take care of itself. Sounds simple, doesn't it? Well, that's because human beings – *all* human beings, not just men – are simple creatures and sometimes our most complicated and confusing thoughts and desires can actually be deconstructed effectively in very straightforward and understandable ways.

Like this one: to have good sex all you need is affection and enthusiasm.

Why tell us that?

The point I'm trying to make is not that sex can and should be perfect every time (I know that isn't true and to believe it can be is wrong) but that in sexual terms, men and women are *not* on different planets.

In *some* ways they are from different worlds – men have smellier feet, aren't as tidy, eat more and watch TV with one hand down their trousers – but not sexually. Our needs, at their most basic level, are, I believe, exactly the same.

You may well know this already. Or at least suspect it. But I want you to know that I know it too before you read the rest of my chapter about sex.

Following on from the affection and enthusiasm lesson, what, then, is the best kind of sex?

That's an easy one: the best kind of sex is the kind you have in a relationship with someone you love.

And remember that's coming from a man.

Single men and sex

When men are single and not getting the best kind of sex or very much at all, many of them will settle for whatever they can get. I know that sounds bad but it's true. The thing is, a lack of sex is bad for our self-esteem. It makes us unhappy, depressed and lonely. Therefore we think getting laid will make us feel better. And sometimes it does, but the effect doesn't last long (much like the sex itself, if we haven't done it for a while).

But in reality, it's not just sex we're missing. The gap in our lives is where affection and emotional intimacy fit. A lack of sex is part of that but not the whole thing. A lack of sex is more like a symptom of that gap rather than a cause. And when men are single, for much of the time they don't quite understand this and so prioritise sex over everything else.

Sexual frustration can warp the male mind.

Men on sex

Here are two quotes about sex from Woody Allen:

'Sex without love is an empty experience. But as empty experiences go, it's one of the best.'

'Love is the answer. But while you're waiting for the answer, sex raises some pretty good questions.'

And here's one from my friend B:

'It is impossible to sleep with too many women.'

See?

Now let's hear a bit more about what B means on this point: 'Single men can't have too much sex. It's impossible. And it's impossible to sleep with too many women. I know because I've tried and all it's proved to me is that an awkward morning is better than a lonely night.'

That is an extreme view but still a useful one because some men are like that some of the time.

'All men want is sex' – not true

The reality is different by one little word. Take away the letters 'i' and 's' and you've got it: all men want sex. And when men are single and not getting enough sex, getting some becomes a priority.

For girls, unless all you're after is a fling, you do not want to be one of the partners who falls into the 'helped me get enough sex until a girlfriend came along' category. I can't guarantee you'll never fall into that category. But you can reduce the chances of it happening.

How?

Most important of all, don't sleep with a guy until you're as sure as you can be that he sees you as more than just a sex-based fling. For more on this, refer to previous chapters.

And now I'll explain a bit more.

Men are very good at having casual sex. This sex is often described as 'meaningless'. But this is misleading. Sex itself is never meaningless, even to a guy who is not looking for anything other than sex. As you now know from the previous few pages, that sex means something to *him* because it makes him feel good and thus is beneficial for his general state of mind. The word 'meaningless' can only be applied to the person he's having it with. She is just a warm, willing body, a blow-up doll with a voice. She might as well not have a name.

This may sound harsh but it is true. And while I accept that many women are capable of having similarly emotion-free sex and seeing men in exactly the same way, I'm not sure many of them would be particularly pleased to be thought of like that. It's not nice. But it happens, all the time.

Girls do casual sex too

I'd just like to make something clear. I don't disapprove of girls having casual sex nor do I think they want it any less than men do. When you're single (either male or female), you have the opportunity to live spontaneously in a way you can't when you're with someone. This can be fun, exciting and wild, and you should make the most of it. I am not, however, encouraging you to go out and sleep with every guy who shows an interest. If you want to spend the night with a hot guy you met half an hour ago, you should feel free to go for it. Just make sure your expectations are realistic and don't do it too often.

See? I'm no prude.

An awkward question

In a rare moment of vulnerability, a guy I know asked me this question: 'Is it possible to be truly happy with a girl who doesn't satisfy you sexually?'

This is something that bothers guys because we know how horrible it feels to be denied sex by someone we love. Because, you see, sex to a guy is not just scratching an itch, it's much more than that. More of which later.

But in the meantime, is it possible for a guy to be truly happy with a girl who doesn't satisfy him sexually?

This isn't a yes or no answer. And that's not another lame attempt to dodge the question. The answer to that question can occasionally be yes or no in some cases but far from all. In most cases, if a guy is with a girl he loves and she doesn't have sex with him often enough, he'll sometimes feel rejected and unhappy and thus unsatisfied. But will he still be truly happy? If he really loves the girl, he might well be. But – and be in no doubt about this – he'd be happier if she had sex with him more.

That doesn't mean reaching new levels of deviancy several times a day. All she has to do is make him feel like she *wants* him and then for both of them to find the frequency that suits them as a couple, whether that's two or three times a week or five times a night. We want to be wanted and to be the lovers our girls used to dream of. That's all there is to it. As I've said before, men are simple creatures.

I realise I'm painting a picture of men as being sex-obsessed. And quite simply that's because we are. Sex is hugely important to us and because we have egos, emotions and urges, that area of our lives can be complicated and sometimes unfulfilling. But I'm also aware that girls can have just as much cause for dissatisfaction.

For example, I know a girl who has been with her guy for a long time, years and years. I also know that she has never had an orgasm with him. That's never, ever. Not even in the first few passion-filled months of their relationship back when they were younger, worked fewer hours under less pressure and pretty well didn't have a care in the world. Not even then.

The issue wasn't that she didn't fancy him, rather that whatever he did wasn't quite right for her. And the result was that she has not had a single orgasm over the entire time they've been together.

Is she truly satisfied sexually? No. But they are married now, so is she happy? Yes, I think she is.

A tip that, if it applies to you, I hope for your sake you follow

That story is tragic. This girl is capable of having orgasms and I'm sure the guy would be capable of giving them to her, but she has never told the guy how to do it for her. So here's a quick, uncomplicated tip for any girl who finds herself in a similar situation. If you're with a guy who you like and the one thing wrong is that he doesn't give you orgasms, then assuming there's something that works for you but he's not doing it, *tell him what to do*. Take the boy to school. Tell him exactly what you like and how you like it to be done. You'll have a better time and he'll be happy too because he'll know he's satisfying you. And please, please, please don't let yourself go the same way this girl did, for the sake of both of you.

What was my reply to that awkward question?

I know it's rude to answer a question with a question but sometimes one has no choice. To do anything else would be too awkward. Being asked the question about whether a guy can be truly happy with a girl who doesn't satisfy him sexually was one of those moments. The conversation went like this:

Him: 'Is it possible to be truly happy with a girl who doesn't satisfy you sexually?'

Me (after some thought and in a serious voice): 'Do you love her?'

Him: 'Yes.'

Me: 'Well there's your answer.'

He seemed happy with that and I was glad the conversation was over.

Finally, the first sex with a guy you like

OK, enough general comments, theories about male and female sexuality and stories. It's business time. Let's go back to the moment where you've decided you're going to sleep with this new guy. Either enough time (at least three dates) has passed or you've had a few drinks and can't wait any longer. Jumping into bed early is, as I've said, totally understandable – I don't think there's anything wrong with giving into your primal urges every now and then whether you're male or female. Just be aware of what you're risking (not just STIs: anything sexual happening before the third date means your chances of being more than a fling get smaller and smaller).

In any case, now you're about to go to bed for the first time with a guy who you like and who likes you. What else do you need to know?

Firstly and most importantly, he will be nervous too – which is why the first time with a new guy you like doesn't matter. As long as nothing goes terribly wrong during the first one, you've both done well. And by terribly wrong I mean so terribly wrong you never want to set eyes on each other again, let alone be naked together.

Minor mishaps involving accidental pain (teeth, for example), poor performance (him being too quick), bodily functions (everyone farts sometimes) or even total failure to stand to attention on his part do not matter at all as long as you don't take things too seriously (how can anyone take all that grunting and face pulling seriously anyway?). Smile, cuddle up to him and say, 'We'll do better next time.' And most of all, be glad the tricky first one is out of the way.

Speaking of him being too quick, let me just explain something about that. The usual reason – ninety-nine times out of 100 – for a guy getting to the finish line before you're even out of the starting blocks is that something has been going on in his mind in the lead-up to the moment.

That might be excitement, especially if it's the first time you've had sex with him. If you've waited a few dates and you know he likes you, then he'll have been looking forward to this moment for some time. The suspense will have built up and he will see you as a something special. He'll have been thinking about how amazing it is that he's going to go to bed with this gorgeous girl he's met. He'll be feeling lucky and proud and horny all at the same time. It's also very likely he won't have had sex with anyone else for a while and thus he'll be very, very excited about sleeping with you. And of course the more excited he is beforehand, well, the quicker it will all be over. We can't help that.

Just remember: that's not an insult.

And anyway, half an hour later he'll be ready, willing and able to get going on round two.

The second reason for an early finish is that on top of all that excitement, he might be nervous (if he likes you he's going to want to impress you), and that might exaggerate the effects of the excitement and bring things to an even swifter conclusion. Again, that is most definitely not an insult. In fact both are the opposite of insults.

So don't expect the world first time round. If you're nice about it, you'll get a bit more the second time and so on.

Remember: practice makes perfect.

Sex and non-single men

This can also happen in relationships. If a couple don't have sex for a few days or a week or more, the chances are that when they do it again, the guy is not going to reach his peak performance because he'll be very sensitive, having not done anything for a while. So if it's his first time in a while, lower your expectations.

And here's some advice: if you want him to last longer, have sex with him more regularly. No, that last sentence was not the result of a male conspiracy to get us laid more often. It's the biological truth. The more we do it, the longer it lasts. Fact.

But fundamentally, as long as you're nice to each other afterwards – talk and cuddle and don't take the sex too seriously – then whatever went wrong (if something did go wrong) won't matter, even if he lasted less time than it takes you to read this sentence. Or even this one.

I'm getting very candid now – sorry, Mum

It is very difficult for a girl to be bad in bed. For a guy to go away from a sexual encounter with a girl he cares about and for him to think they've had good sex, all he needs to know is that she had a good time. If she enjoyed herself, he'll be puffed up and proud and consider it a success.

That is a fact.

Now, knowing all that, can you really tell me men are totally one-dimensional about sex?

This may surprise you too: when you first go to bed with a guy you want to be more than a fling, don't be too naughty too soon. Unless it's something you really, really enjoy, you don't need to pull out amazing sex tricks early on to impress a guy you like. If he really likes you, he'll be so happy to be having sex with you that all you will need to have a great time together are my two old favourites: affection and enthusiasm. You'll be able to gauge where the line is by his reactions to things. If he's enjoying himself (which should be obvious – that's one area where men are definitely not complicated), then carry on. You don't need to keep pushing the boundaries to make a guy like you more. If he likes you, he likes you. And if you've waited a while to sleep with him so he attaches great value to you, then he'll simply be pleased to be naked with you.

Just make sure you enjoy yourself too. There's nothing wrong with being a bit selfish in bed.

Too much too soon?

I know a guy who when he was single slept with as many girls as he could in as many creative and kinky ways as he possibly could. But when he met the girl who would later become his wife, his sexual tastes changed dramatically and now it's missionary position or nothing. Forever. Fair enough, I suppose. But I can't help thinking they're both missing out.

Anyway, the reason why I share this is to show that you don't need to be crazy wild in bed from the very beginning to get a guy interested in you. If he likes you, all you need to do is enjoy yourself. Keep the flashy moves and kinky little turn-ons (if you have them) for later. You don't need them on day one.

It's good to talk

There's one word to add to the 'affection and enthusiasm' list and that word is *communication*.

Men, you see, don't mind being told what to do. If you're giving us knowledge that will help us give you a better time, then most right-thinking, decent guys (and I'm assuming the one you're in bed with is one of those) will be happy to receive instructions.

But how you give those instructions matters. Don't say, 'I love it when guys do this . . .' Instead say 'I love it when you . . .' or 'I'd love it if you . . .' or just 'Do this . . .'

Also, if you say, 'I love it when my [something] is [something] ed,' that will automatically make him think about the previous times your something was somethinged by another guy and whether that other guy did it better than him.

Reminders of your past – whatever it is – at moments like that are not what we want to hear. Tell us what you want in the way you'd like us to tell you what we want.

No matter how many previous boyfriends you've had, your new man will, if he's the insecure type (as most of us are occasionally and especially with girls we like a lot), worry that he compares unfavourably to your previous lovers or be daunted by the idea of you being more experienced than him. That's why, when you give him instructions, you should present them in the right way. A sensitive way.

Equally, if you want to praise him, don't go over the top. We know when we're being spun a line. Words like 'good' and 'great' and 'amazing' can be said or whispered. Theatrical screams aren't necessary. Just relax, be yourself and communicate with him and everything will be fine. Better than fine, actually.

Sex in relationships

Given that this is the chapter about sex at the start of relationships, I want to talk a little bit more about sex in relationships for guys. Basically, what it's like further down the line for men when we're with a girl we love.

Within a relationship, sex is hugely important to us. If our girlfriend or wife doesn't want to have sex then the frustration we feel is not only sexual because that feeling in men is linked to our emotions. 'If she doesn't want to have sex with me, she doesn't love me any more,' runs the usual train of thought. And if it's not that train, it will be the other one, not the disappointing 'she doesn't want to have sex' reason (which can happen for all kinds of reasons), but the ego-crushing 'she doesn't want to have sex *with me*'. That is a horrible, horrible feeling for men to go through.

Even B, that bastion of male insensitivity, understands this. His view is this: 'Men cheat for one reason: sex. But the root of it is not simply that men are one-dimensional sexual beings. Sex is genetically bred into us as our purpose for living. We are here to reproduce, after all. And so if we're single and not getting any, we get upset. But if we're in a relationship with a girl who we love and we're still not getting any, the wounds are much, much deeper. We get *really* upset.'

Remember that was B talking about emotions. That won't happen often. And he's not finished yet. Here's some more of his unusual honesty: 'A man's sexual urge is not as simplistic as being hungry or thirsty, as some people believe. We're far more complicated than that. Sex with our girlfriend makes us happy because we love her and the fact she wants to have sex with us means she feels the same.

'The fact, therefore, is that if a man has enough sex, he's very, very unlikely to look elsewhere. I know that makes us sound like uncivilised jungle beasts but deep down that's what we are. The two keys to stopping a man cheating are to look after him emotionally and physically. That means listening to him and understanding him and having sex with him often enough that he doesn't want it with anyone else.'

So, you see, even the guys who seem the toughest on the outside can be soft in the middle.

A confession from me

I like to read women's magazines. There, I said it. I have always liked them, ever since my older sister first brought home a copy of *Just Seventeen*. My copies of *The Beano* and *Shoot* weren't quite so tempting after I'd had a look through what she was reading. Pictures of girls and articles about sex, or cartoons and football statistics? Not a difficult choice.

These days I read men's magazines far more but I will still not hesitate to pick up publications intended for women if I spot one in the dentist's waiting room or my girlfriend has one. They're goldmines in so many ways.

And that habit enabled me to pick up this gem from a recent issue of *Glamour*. In a feature about how women's sex lives were transformed, the journalist and author Rachel Johnson wrote this: 'Basically bedroom action is the barometer of your relationship; if you're at it like rabbits, you're likely to be on tremendously good terms. It's also the canary in the mine shaft; if sex is tailing off, your couple mojo could be too . . . Like tennis and cooking, sex is 90% enthusiasm and 10% technique . . . Sex is really big in men's lives . . . Men are up for sex most of the time . . . Even when I'm not up for sex (sometimes my headache has lasted for years at a time) I always enjoy it once we get the kayak into the water and start paddling . . . It's always worth staying awake after *Newsnight* in the end . . . and you sleep like a log after.'

There isn't much I can add to that. Sex in relationships can be so complicated, with layers of emotional scars, stress about daily life and insecurities putting up barriers to what should be a simple pleasure between two people who love each other. Rachel Johnson clearly understands that, which is why I reprinted her words.

Humfrey's guide to keeping a boyfriend happy

Feed him, listen to him, talk to him, laugh with him, have sex with him and he will be happy with you.

And that's it. The magic formula. The Holy Grail of Man Handling. Right there in twenty-two words is all you need to know about men.

That special guy

Most guys can't wait to have sex with a girl they like. We're programmed that way – we can't rationalise or control our sexual urges. Very rarely is the She in the blossoming relationship the one whose advances are gently rebuffed until the He feels ready to make that step.

But it does happen.

And it happened to my friend Wendy with a guy called William.

Humfrey Hunter

The tale of William and Wendy and her fight to get him into bed

Wendy met William and they liked each other. Both were in their early thirties and had experienced enough of life to know when a person is worth taking seriously. Each thought the other was worth taking seriously.

Wendy and William went on a few dates. They started liking each other some more. William liked Wendy's sparky personality and her sense of humour. Wendy liked William's sense of humour too, as well as his quiet dignity and intelligence. He was thoughtful and considerate, unlike some of the loud, laddish guys she'd dated unsuccessfully in the past. Best of all, Wendy felt William respected her, something unusual in her experience. He was treating her well.

Four weeks and eight dates later, he was still treating her well. Respectfully. Which Wendy appreciated. But by now she also wanted William to tear her clothes off and show her his slightly less civilised side as well.

But William wouldn't do it. He wanted to wait.

Another month passed and Wendy was beginning to go a little bit crazy. She wanted William so much but he was still holding back. She didn't know what to do.

Then he suggested they go away for the weekend to his friend's cottage in the country.

Bingo. Business time.

Wendy came back from that weekend extremely happy and two years on they're still happily together.

So, you see, not all guys are irresistibly driven to seek sex.

Sounds a bit too good to be true...

Well, yes, I can see that. But that story is 100% factually correct. I should, though, add one other fact: I don't know anyone else who would behave or has behaved like William did. Not me and not anyone else I know. William's the exception and the rest of us are the rule.

At least I'm honest.

MEN SENSE:

1. When you go to bed with a guy you like for the first time, smile, relax and enjoy yourself.
2. In the wider scheme of things (i.e. your developing relationship), the first time you have sex with a new guy doesn't matter. So don't worry about it if something goes wrong. Concentrate on kissing and having lots of eye contact.
3. Look at your first night together as another way to get to know him rather than an opportunity to impress him with your sexual prowess.
4. Don't be afraid to be selfish. Tell him what you like. But do it in a way you'd like *him* to tell *you* what he likes – i.e. sensitively.
5. Make him think you're having a good time. Male sexual confidence is fragile but if you look after it, the results can and will be amazing.

Chapter Seven

Handling a One-Night Stand with Dignity

- What men really think of one-night stands
- Why women shouldn't feel bad if they like them
- Why women shouldn't have too many
- How to stay in control of the situation, before, during and after

Everyone likes having sex and if you're single and don't know where or when you're next going to have it, why not do it whenever you want with whoever you want and – as long as you're safe – to hell with the consequences? It's the twenty-first century, after all.

That's one way of looking at it. Another way is that human beings – both male and female – are essentially the same no matter what century they lived in and that means that while some casual sex is fine (and sometimes much better than that), too much is, well, too much. Deep down we're all looking for one person to love and be loved by and casual sex doesn't help much on that score.

In fact, the upsides of one-night stands – the fun, the post-relationship catharsis, the boost to your self-esteem – only exist if you indulge occasionally.

The two main reasons for me holding that view are these:

1. Anyone who has lots of one-night stands is almost definitely not a happy person and has problems or issues which will not be helped by having more and more casual sex with more and more people; and
2. Very rarely does a one-night stand become a relationship.

To be clear, that was not me moralising. I do not judge anyone negatively for having one-night stands. I'm simply making the point that if a person's number of one-night stands is shooting up, it's very likely their happiness levels are dropping at exactly the same time and at a similar rate – i.e. fast – and casual sex is never the best remedy for that situation, whether you're male or female.

NOTE:
I am treating guys and girls exactly the same way in this chapter. I am not going to get into the genetic differences between us and why men might be more suited to one-night stands than women.

The alcohol question – how many one-night stands would happen if alcohol had never been invented?

The thing about alcohol and girls that I've never quite got my head round is whether alcohol gets rid of girls' inhibitions – i.e. makes them do things they want to do deep down but are too worried about the consequences to do sober – or makes them do things they would never do sober. I don't think I'll ever fully understand. For guys I think more often than not it's the first of those two, although some of us wouldn't admit that. Whether you're male or female, it's easy to blame alcohol for something you've done. But is the booze an excuse or a reason?

If a single person gets drunk, sleeps with someone and then regrets it – and I mean truly regrets it, not when they pretend to save face because they're a little bit embarrassed – my advice is simple: don't get so drunk in future. It's not complicated.

Next (slightly unrelated) question: does alcohol excuse infidelity?

No, I don't think it does. At some stage in the build-up to the actual act of infidelity, drunken or not, whoever does the cheating will think about their boyfriend or girlfriend and make a decision: either I'm not going to let this happen because of him/her or I know I'm in a relationship with him/her but I'm going to do this anyway. Just because whoever does the cheating doesn't remember this thought process happening doesn't make it forgivable. After all, it still happened. And exactly the same rules apply for guys and girls.

What guys think of one-night stands

We men are inherently lazy. We like short cuts and paths of least resistance. And we men also love sex. In fact we are automatically driven to seek it, compelled to find willing women by forces within us that we don't understand and can't control.

Therefore most single guys would consider a night of going out, meeting a girl and sleeping with her to be a successful evening. So we like one-night stands. We get to have sex without having to go through any of the uncertainty and expensive and time-consuming hassle of dating someone. All we had to do was go out, dance a bit, drink a bit and talk a bit and away we went.

What could possibly be better than that?

Actually, there is one thing that is better than that: having sex with a girl we really like. Or even love.

What guys think of girls who have one-night stands

If we have a one-night stand with a girl and never see her again we will generally have good, if vague, memories of her. But these positive feelings will never stretch to thinking of her as a potential girlfriend (I don't know of a single couple who weren't friends already who got together after a one-night stand).

That said, we won't think this girl was a slag or morally bankrupt in any way. The male train of thought will be something like, 'She met me and wanted to sleep with me a few hours later and who can blame her for that?'

No man will criticise anyone for wanting to sleep with him, unless he's a homophobe who's just been chatted up by another man, in which case his opinion doesn't count anyway. So there's no moralising or judging going on in that context.

The flipside of that coin is what happens when a girl we like tells us she's had lots of one-night stands in the past.

We do not like hearing that. In fact we hate hearing it.

But before you start thinking men are hypocrites, let me add one thing: very few men will judge a girl negatively for something like this. We might be a bit grumpy for a while but we'll deal with it. You see, most of us make rational decisions to treat girls as we hope they treat us. And that means we won't judge her on what happened before we met on the understanding that she won't hold our pasts against us either. Only what has happened since we got together counts.

Of course that doesn't change the basic fact that we still don't like hearing that a girl we like has slept around. The reason, simply, is to do with us men and our egos, not you.

One-night stand story #1

Eddie went out one night and met two girls, Elspeth and Emily. One of Eddie's friends was going out with a friend of the girls and the trio met when two groups met up in the same club. It was late and everyone was drunk.

Eddie was feeling frisky. He'd recently broken up with a girl and felt like trying his luck with the ladies again (it wasn't a traumatic break-up). He met Elspeth and Emily and immediately formed his opinion of both. Emily was gorgeous and obviously not going to succumb to his charms easily. Elspeth, while not unattractive, was not in Emily's league.

But Elspeth was much more forward than Emily.

Can you guess which one Eddie ended up going home with?

The next morning

Eddie woke up early and in an unfamiliar bed. Elspeth's bed. In his own words: 'I was drunk, OK? Emily was obviously hotter and more of a challenge and under normal circumstances, if I was sober, I'd have been much more interested in her than Elspeth. But Elspeth made it really easy for me. I'd barely talked to her before she was standing with her face inches away from mine. Of course I kissed her. I was way too drunk to even contemplate doing anything else. I took the easy option.'

The next morning, Eddie left Elspeth's house feeling slightly worse for wear. There were no great dramas while he was there and from what I can gather they both had a good time. At least, that's what he said. The upshot was he took her number and later that day texted her. 'I didn't want to date her,' Eddie said, 'but she was a friend of a friend and a nice girl so I wanted to be respectful. And she was funny so I thought some hungover banter might be amusing.'

Fair enough? I think so.

Eddie texted Elspeth that evening with some witticism referring to how terrible he felt. Elspeth replied saying he should have stayed in bed with her rather than running away so early. Eddie texted back saying she was probably right and that he should come back to her bed some time soon (he was feeling a bit flirtatious after Elspeth's message about staying in her bed).

Fair enough? Again, I think so, for both of them.

But then Elspeth did something Eddie wasn't expecting. Her next message said: 'Ha ha! You'll have to take me out on a few interesting dates before you get in there again!'

To which Eddie replied: 'Ha ha! That's a shame,' and that was it. Later he said this to me: 'What was she thinking? Did she really expect me to want to take her out for a few dates so we could have sex again when she'd already slept with me barely three hours after we met? No way. What would be the point?'

To be clear, Eddie wasn't criticising Elspeth for sleeping with him so quickly. Rather, he couldn't understand what logic had gone on in her head which led her to think that this kind of first meeting would be a precursor to 'a few interesting dates'. If they'd done nothing but kiss on that first night then maybe Elspeth would have been in the right and Eddie would have been happy to take her out. But not after a one-night stand.

One-night stand story #2 –
the easiest lesson to learn

Here's another one. A girl said this to me: 'I met a guy at a club on a Saturday night, slept with him and the next morning he took my number and said he'd call. I didn't hear from him again until about 11 p.m. the next Friday night when he texted to see if I was out near him. Why didn't he call me? Does he like me? And should I see him again? Does he want to be my boyfriend?'

I said this to her: 'He is not interested in you as a person. You will never be his girlfriend. Because you had sex with him on the night you met, all you are to him now is someone to have sex with. That's all. In his mind any relationship between you is founded on and defined by sex. I'm sure he does like you, but that's because you had sex with him. He might well think you're pretty too but that's irrelevant. Why isn't he interested in who you are? Simple: he doesn't know your personality and the chances are he isn't interested in it either, seeing as you've already slept with him. Should you see him again? Only if you're interested in casual sex because that's all you're ever going to get from him.'

The fact is, when sex has been offered up that quickly, there's no way of turning the situation into something more romantic than carnal. I don't know anyone who's ended up going out with a girl who slept with them so quickly. Of course I know couples who had sex on the night of the first *date*, but not on the day they first met. They exist, I'm sure of that too, it's just I don't know any of them.

Basic guidelines

The same rules apply to one-night stands as the rest of your dating life. They are: be confident, be clear about what you want, don't be shy, don't be embarrassed and be true to yourself. If you start feeling awkward, either stop yourself feeling awkward or go home. Unless you're cheating on someone or sleeping with a guy who's in a relationship with a friend of yours, you have nothing to be ashamed of or embarrassed about, which means that whatever you want to do is fine. If you want to go back to a guy's house, have sex with him and then get a taxi home straight away, that's your prerogative and privilege.

The trick to maintaining your dignity before, during or after a one-night stand is to not be embarrassed or self-conscious at any stage. This can be tricky and is where (a little) alcohol can be useful to help shake off inhibitions. Just don't make a habit of waking up next to guys who look like frogs rather than princes.

How many is too many?

I don't know, because numbers don't matter. The answer is entirely down to individuals and so only you can answer that question. If you're happy (I mean truly happy – not able to convince yourself and your friends that you're happy) then you don't need to make changes in your life. But if you're not happy then maybe you should alter the way you're behaving.

Should single guys and girls make the most of their single days?

Yes, of course they should. But making the most of your single days doesn't necessarily mean sleeping with as many people as possible. Making the most of your single days means having adventures and being happy, doing what you want to do and finding out things about yourself. Those things might be to do with your sexual tastes and habits but they could also be an interest in amateur dramatics, marathon running or dancing on Asian beaches as the sun rises. Whatever makes *you* happy.

One-night stand morning-after protocol

1. Phone numbers

If you don't want a guy's number after spending the night with him, that's fine. And if you don't want him to have your number then that's perfectly acceptable too. But if he makes no effort whatsoever to either get your number or give you his, then he's an idiot. That is not good manners.

2. Leaving

If you wake up at a guy's house after a one-night stand, unless he's very, very welcoming and offers you breakfast or a cup of tea, then it's very likely he would rather you left. I'm not saying you should leave before you're ready (you might want some more sleep, for example, in which case snooze for as long as you want). I'm simply pointing out that most guys feel awkward and uncomfortable in this situation and that's not going to make you happy either. I know a guy who pretended he was going to play golf at 9 a.m. one morning to get a girl to leave his flat. He dressed up in his golf clothes, got his clubs and kit together, put it all in his car and left. The problem was he then had to wait until a bus had come before he could go home because the stop was right outside his house. So he sat round the corner watching from behind a bush until she'd gone. Classy. I know another guy who went back to a girl's house from a club, had sex with her and then when she went to the toilet straight afterwards, he gathered up his clothes and ran out of the house. Before she'd even come back into her room. There is a minority of guys who will behave like that but most won't. Most, including me, think that is very bad form indeed.

3. Embarrassed? Don't be

Be relaxed and chilled out. If he's a nice-looking guy or you had a good time together (hopefully both will be true), don't be embarrassed or awkward. Relax. So you slept with a guy you fancied? What's the big deal? There isn't one. Have a nice chat the next morning, leave politely, and chalk it up to experience.

The story that made me blush

When I started writing my column, it was the perfect excuse to make all kinds of big promises about being the man who never said no. I vowed to do anything, any time, anywhere, no matter what it was. I talked a big, big game. But I didn't actually play one. In the end, about the most crazy thing I did was get hypnotised, which was fun but entirely undramatic. First, though, here's the story of the biggest 'no' I said.

I was by the bar at a media drinks party when I started chatting to the woman next to me. She was attractive – not gorgeous but definitely attractive – and immaculately pre- sented, dark-haired and slim in a tight black dress.

She was also very flirty and wearing a wedding ring.

No problem, I thought, a bit of cheeky banter might be harmless fun. Then her husband turned up. He introduced himself and the fun chat continued.

In fact, if anything she was a little more flirty than she had been earlier, stroking my arm and giving me lots of eye contact. Odd as that felt to me, her husband didn't seem to mind so I assumed that was just her way.

The chat carried on merrily. I told them about life as a single man in London and they laughed at my column stories in that smug and slightly patronising way happily married people do when listening to single people's tales. We talked about work and it turned out they ran a company in a business not unrelated to something I was doing at the time.

Then her husband asked me: 'Would you like to join us?'

This took me by surprise. 'That's a bit quick,' I replied, 'We only met twenty minutes ago and you haven't even seen my CV yet. But maybe. Shall I come to your office for a chat some time?'

They looked at each other and grinned.

'No,' the lady said, now pressing her chest against my arm and stroking the back of my neck. 'That's not what he means. Would you like to join us tonight? At home.'

With that, she kissed me gently on the cheek and the penny dropped. I blushed the deepest shade of red it is humanly possible to go. Thankfully it was quite dark so they couldn't see my scarlet face.

'That's not really my kind of thing,' I spluttered, trying desperately to sound cool.

'Why not?' said the woman, pushing herself against me, 'Don't you like me?'

'Of course I like you,' I insisted, not wanting to offend her but by now desperate to be somewhere else. 'It's just your husband. He's a bit too, well, male for my liking.'

Then she whispered in my ear: 'Oh, he's totally straight. It's only me who wants you. He'll just watch.'

I'm not judgmental about what people get up to in private. Not at all. But something about being propositioned like this made me very, very uncomfortable. I did not want to be part of this married couple's sex game and I felt completely out of my depth. I said no thanks and scurried off to the loo like a scared child.

When I finally got up the courage to show my face in the party again I saw the couple talking to another guy. He looked happy rather than scared. I silently wished him luck and went home.

MEN SENSE:

1. Choose your one-night stand partner carefully – that means you shouldn't be too drunk when you have one.

2. Keep your expectations realistic. Sex is on the menu, not a relationship.

3. If you want to leave at any point, just leave. And if you want him to go, tell him to go. But be polite – men have feelings too.

4. If you go to his place, don't leave anything important behind. Whether or not you forgot your watch/make-up/jacket accidentally, it will look like you did it on purpose.

5. If he leaves something at yours, that's fine. If you notice while he's there and want to see him again, don't say anything. It's a good excuse to contact him again and what have you got to lose?
6. Don't leave without saying goodbye. You wouldn't be happy if he did that, would you?
7. If you're at your place and want him to leave, tell him.
8. If you're at your place, don't ever worry about what he thinks regarding how tidy it is. That soooo doesn't matter.
9. If you never hear from him again, don't be surprised.
10. If you hear from him late at night again, all he wants is sex. Go back to tip number 2.
11. Be careful. Always.

Chapter Eight

When Friends Become Lovers

- Why friends should have flings
- Why friends shouldn't have flings
- How to manage everyone's expectations
- Why he's not the right fling for you
- How to get what you want by doing nothing

When two friends try to become more than friends, the result is sometimes good, sometimes bad, sometimes very good, sometimes very bad and sometimes somewhere in the middle.

Insightful? Maybe not on the first reading.

But right? Yes.

I will use examples of true stories to prove my point. With made-up names in helpfully alphabetical order . . .

Story A – the good

Alice and Andrew were friends for years. They were part of the same circle and saw each other regularly. They got on well and while there was undeniably chemistry between them, there was never a time when both were single, so the feelings each secretly harboured for the other remained unspoken.

But eventually a time came when they were both single. Alice had broken up with her long-term boyfriend eighteen months earlier and was enjoying her single life when Andrew's relationship ended.

Suddenly things changed and the unspoken attraction between them became spoken. Who did the speaking doesn't matter (I don't actually know anyway). The fact it was done is what counts.

So what happened next? Did a passionate affair explode into their lives before the flames disappeared, leaving only charred emotional wreckage, like a plane crash or something else dramatic and devastating?

No.

Not by a long shot.

At the stage of their lives when all this was happening (late twenties and early thirties), the pair were mature and wise enough not to fall into the trap of letting lust override logic. Both cared deeply about the other and thought their strong feelings could become something serious. But Andrew was wary because he had just come out of a relationship. He didn't want Alice to be a rebound fling because he cared about and respected her too much. And Alice was worried for exactly the same reason because she knew everything about Andrew's recently ended relationship.

Alice and Andrew were honest with each other and talked very openly about the situation, which included him telling her that while he *thought* he had serious feelings for her because every part of him was telling him she was very, very special, he couldn't be sure his perception of his own emotions hadn't been warped by the recent break-up.

Alice understood how dangerous her position was but even so, while they didn't start sleeping together, they did spend time as a couple away from their friends. They couldn't help themselves. During that time Alice inevitably started falling for Andrew in a big, big way and a month or so later she told him things couldn't carry on as they were, with her not knowing if there was any chance at all of them being together at some point. Alice decided she needed to protect herself so she told Andrew she didn't want to see him for at least a month.

Andrew's reaction was, I am pleased to say, not that of the immature male who decides he wants something as soon as he is told he can't have it. Instead, he respected her wishes and backed off (which made her friends like him because again he was very obviously doing the right thing).

Despite Andrew's good intentions, Alice was then left in a horrible emotional limbo. She knew that, in effect, she'd sent him away to decide if he really was interested in her or not, which meant in a few weeks he might well come back with open arms. But equally, he might not come back at all. So for Alice it was all or nothing, and worst of all there was now nothing she could do to affect Andrew's decision.

Actually, there was something Alice could do. And that something was . . . nothing.

Nothing?

Yes, nothing.

You see, by doing nothing she didn't put any pressure on him and she didn't come across as clingy or desperate, which is not attractive. She didn't 'do nothing' (that double negative was deliberate) specifically for that reason, mind you. She did nothing because she is a wise, honest, emotionally intelligent, confident girl who doesn't play games and likes to keep her dignity intact.

And that is precisely why, when the month was up, Andrew couldn't wait to see her again.

The art of doing nothing successfully

Doing nothing was not really doing *nothing*, if you see what I mean. Doing nothing was a clever tactic. It put the ball in Andrew's court and made him think about what he wanted. It also may have sowed seeds of doubt in his mind because Alice told him she had accepted it was possible he would not want her. She was prepared for that eventuality and this kind of maturity is impressive to us simple male creatures. She'd made her views clear and now she wasn't going to put any pressure on him to make up his mind.

The most important point is this: Alice kept as much control as she possibly could. Also, she was true to herself because she made sure Andrew knew how she felt about him. That takes strength and, as I've said already, wisdom. Which we men admire.

To be honest, how Alice managed to keep a lid on her emotions for that month and not contact him I'll never know. I respect her incredibly for that. And it may well be that even if she hadn't kept her cool, Andrew would still have come running (I like to think so). But we'll never know. What we do know, however, is that Alice is a bright girl who did exactly the right things at the right times.

One more point: this story makes Alice sound like an

ice queen, a calculating, emotionless girl. But I know her well and she's nothing like that. She is warm, wise and self-respecting. Andrew is kind and respectful to her and they are now very happy.

MORALS OF THE STORY:
- *There are good guys out there (at least one, anyway).*
- *Doing nothing is sometimes the right thing to do.*

Story B, part one – the bad

Bob is twenty-seven. He has a friend, Beatrice, who is twenty-six. They were at university together and are best friends. They hang out together at weekends, talk all the time and are very, very close.

Bob and Beatrice have never even kissed each other. But Bob is deeply infatuated with Beatrice. In fact, he thinks he's in love with her. Every time he sees her, it's torture for him. They function successfully as friends but he wants more. So much more.

Has Beatrice ever given him a sign that she felt the same? Bob's not sure. She is always pleased to see him, wants to spend time with him and she obviously has fun with him. What does that mean? Bob doesn't know.

Poor Bob.

Bob agonises for months and months about what to do. All his friends know what's going on and suspect she's not interested. Her friends probably know as well and probably think the same. But no one gives him any clear-cut advice about what to do. They think it's unlikely she's going to be interested and don't want him to be disappointed but they also can't stand seeing him so unhappy, with no end in sight for the loveless purgatory he's going through. It's tricky for them.

While this is going on, Bob has relationships with other girls but they're always half-hearted and he always ends up letting the girls down because none of them is Beatrice and so they don't measure up to her.

What, then, should Bob do?

Bob wallowed in his misery for longer than he should have, became even more frustrated and unhappy and finally – *finally* – decided to do something positive. He told Beatrice how he felt. Which was, in my opinion, absolutely the right thing to do. He needed to know what Beatrice thought so he could either start something non-platonic with her or begin the process of moving on.

What happened?

Beatrice wasn't interested and Bob had to start moving on.

Poor Bob again.

Story B, part two – where our 'bad' story turns 'good'

What? How could this possibly suddenly become a 'good' story? Hasn't Bob just had his heart broken?

Good question.

Here's the even better answer.

Yes, Bob has had his heart broken. But broken hearts mend and by telling Beatrice how he felt, Bob helped his begin to heal.

First of all, he kept as much control of the situation (there's that phrase again) as he possibly could. Emotions are impossible to control totally but he did the right thing in what was a very difficult situation for him. The result was he could start to get over Beatrice because he now had to accept that nothing was ever going to happen between them. Full stop, end of story, curtain goes down, dead-end, no second chances, nothing. They would never be together.

For Bob that must have been hard, I know, but infinitely preferable to carrying on indefinitely as he was before.

And guess what happened a few months later, when Bob was well on his way to putting Beatrice behind him?

That's right, he met a girl. *The* girl for him, in fact.

And that is why it's a 'good' story.

Bob was brave, went for what he wanted, faced the facts when he was rejected and then got on with his life in a positive way.

MORAL OF THE STORY:
If you like someone and you don't know if they feel the same, it's far better to find out they don't and start getting over that person than to carry on obsessing over them.

Story C – the very good

Calvin and Clementine met at work. For years they were good friends. She was in a long, long-term relationship (nine years – anything over one year is 'long' in my book) while he was in a couple of less long ones. Calvin and Clementine were close throughout this time.

Then Clementine broke up with her boyfriend and soon afterwards she realised she had feelings for Calvin that were rather stronger than she had previously thought. And Calvin was now single too, which meant opportunity had come knocking.

One day, Clementine, brave girl that she is, summoned up the courage to tell Calvin how she felt (round of applause from me for that). She sat him down, laid her heart on the table and . . . had it thrown back in her face. Calvin said he wasn't interested in her like that. She was his friend and that was all.

Clementine was understandably terribly upset by this and asked Calvin to not be in touch for a while because it would be too hard for her to see him. Of course, Calvin said. He cared about Clementine very much and didn't want to make her feel any worse than she already did (he felt huge guilt for causing her that pain).

About three weeks later, after no contact between the pair of them, Calvin was driving in his car and he passed a park where a couple of months previously he had spent a fun afternoon with Clementine, relaxing in the sunshine. He smiled at the memory as his mind transported him back to that day . . .

Then his mood changed dramatically as an image of the two of them chatting and dozing in the summer heat gave way to one of the last time he saw Clementine, when she was showing him out of her house after he'd dashed her hopes that they might get together. He saw her face again, fighting back tears and hardly able to look at him.

These two memories swirled around in Calvin's head for a few moments until they settled down and when they did it was as if the pieces of a jigsaw had fallen into place.

'What have I done?' Calvin thought. 'What the hell have I done? What if it's too late?' And he nearly crashed his car.

There was no time to lose. Too much had passed already.

Calvin called Clementine and asked where she was.

'At home,' she said.

Calvin said he was ten minutes' drive away.

Three speed-limit-breaking minutes later, he rang her bell.

Clementine opened the door and ... well, he didn't tell me what happened next because Calvin is a gentleman. But it's not hard to work out what went on because eight months later Calvin proposed to Clementine and they are now happily married.

I love that story.

MORALS OF THE STORY:

- *Fairytales do happen.*
- *Taking risks can pay off.*

Story D – the very bad

Derek and Doris met at work. Doris had a boyfriend and was quite a serious girl. Derek was a couple of years younger than Doris and a joker. They got on well and were fond of each other.

Then Doris broke up with her boyfriend and Derek started paying her more attention. A different kind of attention. One that made his intentions clear.

After some soul-searching on her behalf, they started seeing each other. Doris knew she was only recently out of a relationship but Derek was a nice guy. They were friends so she could trust him, right?

Wrong.

About three weeks later, after Doris and Derek had spent a few nights together, he decided he wasn't interested after all. Doris was furious. She felt hurt and deeply let down by Derek. Why did he behave like that?

Unfortunately Derek was either not very grown-up or just the kind of guy who once he's had a girl, loses interest. He might do this consciously (in other words he might get off on chasing after a girl until she succumbs to his advances and then moving on to the next one) or he might do it time after time without really understanding why. I expect it's the second one. He didn't seem deceitful to me, just a bit useless. Perhaps he was simply too young and afraid of commitment to realise what was there in front of him.

I'm afraid quite a lot of guys are like this and Doris was unlucky to fall straight into the trap.

How to avoid the trap

It's impossible to be 100% certain but there are a few indicators you can look for when thinking about whether or not a male friend should become more than that. As I said, these signs aren't proof positive, just useful indicators.

There are three: age, history and instinct.

Age: Is he young? Is he either in his early or mid-twenties or at least a couple of years younger than you? If the answer to either of those is 'yes' then he's in the most likely age group to be one of these unreliable guys. It might be best to keep him as a friend, not allow him to become a lover.

History: Has he either never had a long-term girlfriend, had one he's recently broken up with or never been single for very long in his adult life before now? If the answer to any of those is 'yes' then he might not be a good bet for a long-term relationship with you now.

Instinct: This one's tricky, as Doris found out. What do your instincts tell you about him? Is he a good guy? Does he mean what he says? Do you feel like you can trust him? If the answer to these questions is 'yes' then it's possible he's *not* one of the guys to watch out for. Only possible, though.

What would have happened if Doris asked herself those three questions about Derek before she got involved with him? She would have ticked the 'yes' box all three times. He was single for the first time since he was eighteen, and he was still only twenty-four, so two years younger than her. Both bad signs. Yes, she liked and trusted him, that's true. But with two out of three 'warning signs', she should have kept their friendship as it was.

This is what makes me think he didn't treat her badly on purpose. I'd call him a muppet rather than a bastard, someone who doesn't mean to treat girls badly but ends up doing it anyway. He thought he knew what he wanted – Doris – but then something in his mind told him to run away when it seemed like they might commit to each other.

A guy of his age with his lack of experience of the single life will almost certainly have heard a voice in his head say, 'There might be something better for you out there,' when he looked at Doris, no matter what she was like. He knew she was an amazing girl but deep in his subconscious there was a nagging thought he couldn't quite put his finger on, insistent enough to make him not want to get involved. And that thought was the fantasy that somewhere in the world there's a supermodel waiting for him.

How men grow up (yes, it's true)

As guys get older, they learn what's real and what isn't, which means that if Derek had been two years older than Doris and thus had four more years' experience, he might have realised girls like her don't come along that often. As a result he would have made her his before someone else got the chance to sweep her away.

But he was too young and lacking in wisdom to realise the value of what was in front of him.

Even if Doris *was* actually a supermodel the outcome would have been the same, because at that stage of his life, Derek hadn't met enough girls to know how great she really was.

This happens all the time. I've done it. I don't mean to say I have any regrets, rather that I've got involved with girls and then run away at the first sign of it becoming something serious for no reason I could put my finger on. Every guy has. We can't help doing it and it doesn't make us bad people, it's simply a sign that we have some growing up to do.

For girls who've been hurt this way, that bit of knowledge is probably no consolation whatsoever. But that is how we work. Sometimes guys are messed with by their own minds and we can't help being like that.

Remember, *if this happens to you it's not your fault and there is nothing wrong with you.* In fact, to have a guy do that to you is almost a compliment because in effect what he's saying is that you're the kind of girl he could see himself with for a long time but he just doesn't want to meet you *right now.*

(By the way, if this happens to you over and over again, it *is* your fault and you need to start dating a different kind of guy. I'll tell you what to do about that in another chapter.)

Doris again

Doris didn't hate Derek for what he did. She understood him. But that didn't change the consequences for her: she was hurt and let down at a time in her life when she was very, very vulnerable, and as a result a long time passed before she let her guard down with anyone else. A long, long time. Which is very sad because Doris is an amazing girl.

I don't think she needed to let Derek's behaviour get to her so much. Doris might have understood Derek but what she didn't get, and what made her take so long to get over him, was that it wasn't *personal.* Any girl who met Derek at that moment in his life would have been treated like that. In fact, I'd bet good money she wasn't the only one who suffered in that way. But Doris took it personally when she shouldn't have, because it wasn't.

Behaviour like Derek's is almost always more about the guy involved and his own mind rather than the girl. That's the case 99% of the time. Remember that. It's not you, it's him.

The *other* kind of guy

Derek did not deliberately set out to seduce Doris and then move on once he'd had his fun. But some guys do behave like that. Unfortunately it's very hard to spot or stop them, especially when emotions are making you more vulnerable than usual.

If you doubt someone's motives towards you, watch out for signs I've already mentioned above, such as making a mental note of their romantic history – men, like leopards, very rarely change their spots. Also, notice if they are too smooth and confident (that is always the big one).

But one thing is true no matter if the guy who does this is a muppet like Derek or a bastard like any number of others. That thing is this: *it's nothing personal*. So don't blame yourself. Dust yourself down and move on. Learn from your mistakes. And whatever you do, don't let the behaviour of one idiot stop you from meeting someone else who isn't a muppet or a bastard. There are some good guys out there.

As I said, this has happened before to countless girls and will, I'm sorry to say, keep on happening. Just remember what I've told you about how to give yourself the best possible chance of it not happening to you.

MORAL OF THE STORY:
Men can be idiots. Especially young men. So be wise.

One more thing – the one that will always make you feel better

I told Doris the following story to cheer her up. Did it work? Not really. But at least she knew someone else was worse off than she was.

Anyway, here's the story.

Everyone has a favourite dating disaster story to tell and while I've heard a lot in my time, not even I can remember one that comes even close to this in terms of the sheer scale of the disaster involved. It also shows that girls are perfectly capable of behaving just as badly as men. Actually, make that worse. Read on to find out why.

My friend Ben met a girl called Beth through mutual friends and they clicked immediately. Ben and Beth went on a few dates and had a great time. A couple of weeks later they were regularly spending nights together and it appeared a wonderful relationship was blossoming.

Then Ben took Beth to a good friend's party. Ben didn't know many people going but they were a fun crowd and he wanted to catch up with his mate and spend the evening with his new girlfriend (for she was his girlfriend now).

The party started well; they had a few drinks and met some interesting new people. Beth got a little overenthusiastic with the booze but Ben wasn't particularly worried. After all, it's only ever a matter of time before you get embarrassingly smashed in front of a new love interest. He simply smiled because it was Beth who would go first.

At around 11 p.m., Ben went to get drinks for himself and Beth, leaving her talking to their new friends. A minute later he

181

returned to find her snogging the face off one of the guys they'd just met. Ben reacted calmly, blaming the demon drink. He tapped her on the shoulder and gave her the glass. Beth thanked him politely, put the drink down and then resumed snogging the other guy, at which point Ben was too shocked to do anything other than stand and watch. A few minutes later they went home together.

Not Beth and Ben, but Beth and the other guy.

I cannot imagine how Ben felt. In the end, Beth spent the night with this guy and Ben went home, alone and humiliated. But that wasn't the end of it. Beth spent the next week calling him constantly, begging forgiveness, saying she was mortified by her behaviour and it wouldn't happen again. Ben rightly told her to stick it where the sun doesn't shine. Really, how could she possibly expect a second chance after that?

The only good thing about this sordid tale – and thus the only positive thing I can take away from it – is that I'm glad it happened to someone other than me. So, next time you have a date that ends atrociously, think of Ben and be grateful you weren't in his shoes. And if that doesn't make you feel better about whatever happened to you, nothing ever will.

The rest

I could have filled this whole book with stories about how flings between friends didn't work out. But then I could just as easily fill a million books with stories about how flings between strangers didn't work out. The principle involved in both situations is exactly the same: two people start seeing each other and either it works out or it doesn't. Simple.

What use were friends to me when I was single?

Until I met Charlotte at a friend of mine's wedding, not much, to be brutally honest. In fact, at times they made the whole thing worse.

Of course, there were times when I thought being single was pretty cool. The independence, the excitement of not knowing what was going to happen, who I might meet and when I might meet them.

But there were also times when it wasn't so fun, and there was one particular week when being single really wasn't all that. It started when I got a phone call from a friend of mine, Anne, who was also single.

We were having a good catch-up when she said: 'Humfrey, will you be my back-up? I just watched the episode of *Friends* where they all agree to marry each other if they're still single in ten years. I realised I don't have anyone to do that with so I thought I'd ask you.'

Amazingly, she thought I'd be flattered.

Wrong.

My pride was hurt for two reasons. First, all I was worthy of in her eyes was being a back-up. And second, Anne thought I'd still be single in ten years. Nice to know a friend has so much faith in me. So I turned her down – I'm not being anyone's back-up.

Next, a couple of days later, I was at a friend's birthday party. I was having a good night, nothing particularly debauched, when a girl came up to me and said: 'I hear you're the last single one of the group, so I thought I should come and talk to you because I'm single too.'

She was an attractive girl – tall and blonde – so in theory this should have been a very welcome introduction. I always respect girls who say hello to guys they don't know. But not this time.

The only reason she was talking to me was that I was single, and I was not in the mood for the kind of conversation based purely on that – I mean, couldn't she think of anything else to say? On another day when I was in a different mood I might well have felt differently about her approach but her timing was terrible.

How *not* to meet the future Mrs H

Remember B, the worst man in the world? Well, given how low my morale was after these two incidents, I thought I'd go out for an evening with him. I wasn't expecting to meet any girls (I was not optimistic about pulling at this stage) but I knew that if nothing else the evening would bring some laughs.

After a couple of drinks B started talking to two very fit blondes who I'll call Girl One and Girl Two. B was obviously interested in Girl One and so expected me to entertain Girl Two while he went through his moves. Even though chatting up a girl was about the last thing I felt like doing, I didn't mind being his wing man because he'd do the same for me.

Then, great news – I wasn't actually going to have to chat up Girl Two at all. She was wearing an engagement ring so we'd be able to chat without that extra pressure you get when two people are sizing each other up for a potential date/shag/marriage/whatever.

B and Girl One were getting on very well so Girl Two and I

ended up chatting for a long time. I asked about her fiancé and she told me how they met and so on.

I'll cut to the moment when the conversation got interesting. That moment came shortly after Girl Two said this: 'Our main problem is that he's away for weeks on end with work.'

'That must be difficult,' I said.

'It is. Speaking on the phone makes it easier. But what I really miss I can't get on the phone.'

The interesting bit is coming up now . . .

She looked me in the eyes and said: 'But you could give it to me. Would you be interested in spending time together on a no-strings-attached basis? Just sex, nothing else.'

Now, if you've read the rest of this book you'll know I have a rule about getting involved with girls who aren't single: don't do it. Ever.

Look back at two particular stories in the chapter containing The Big Mistake story if you want to know why. I'd decided long before that I was never going to let something like that happen again so there was no chance of me getting involved with this girl. I told her this and she looked shocked. Apparently she'd never been turned down before.

Perhaps unsurprisingly, conversation was a bit awkward after that. Luckily B and Girl One soon decided to go on to a club together so there was an easy chance for me and Girl Two to leave separately without causing him any problems. But she didn't give up.

The next day, Girl Two Facebooked me to say if I changed my mind, the offer would stay open. But I didn't take her up on it.

A bit of 'What if...?'

It's obvious why I didn't want to get involved with Girl Two – I didn't want to get caught up in another messy situation. I knew by now that if I were going to get involved with a girl she would have to have no baggage. And a fiancé is *big* baggage.

But looking back, I can't help wondering what would have happened if I'd met Girl Two a few months earlier, when I was happy with casual arrangements. Would I have turned her down so readily? A hot girl offering me meaningless, no-strings-attached sex?

Perhaps not. No, make that probably not. And then what? Would Girl Two and I have lived happily ever after? Or would Girl Two's fiancé have tracked me down and pulled out my fingernails with rusty pliers? I have no idea. But however it ended, I'm pretty sure the story wouldn't have been straightforward.

I'm glad I turned her down.

Conclusions

By the very nature of the dating process (girls/guys kiss a few frogs before they find their prince/princess), there are many, many more stories of failed flings than of everlasting love. This is true whether romance happens between two friends-since-they-played-together-as-toddlers or a couple whose first meeting was lecherously rubbing up against each other on a sweaty dancefloor at 1 a.m. after a few too many vodka and Red Bulls.

In general, it doesn't matter what the background to a

couple starting to date looks like. The spectrum of possible outcomes is always the same: either it will work out or it won't.

And that's why I wouldn't advise anyone against dating a friend. I would say, though, that you should only do it if you think it might turn into something serious. Starting a casual fling with a friend when you know it's only ever going to be a casual fling is without doubt a bad idea simply because one of the two people involved will end up wanting more. One or the other of you will have let things start because you're a bit lonely and bored or you see it as an easy way to get sex (that's usually the guy's reason, unless he's been secretly in love with the girl for years). If you think you're on the receiving end of this situation, get out quickly. The longer it goes on, the more he'll think he can get away with treating you like that and the more hurt you'll be when it ends, which it most definitely will. And if you're the one who sees it as simply an easy way to get sex, then stop taking advantage of your friend. It's not fair.

But if dating a friend turns into something serious, then the chances are you'll have something brilliant. And if that's the possible prize, take a risk.

To sum up, then, two out of the four possible scenarios had endings that weren't entirely negative. What does that tell us? It tells us that when I made my thoroughly un-insightful opening statement in this chapter, I was absolutely right: sometimes turning friendship into more works, sometimes it doesn't.

If you add my own story – The Big Mistake – from Chapter Two into the mix, then the odds are slightly in favour of it not working. But that, as I explained earlier, is the way with all kinds of dating.

One final word

When I was writing my dating column, occasionally readers would email me asking for advice on their own dating lives. One week I decided to offer myself up as a dating advice service to see what material came my way. Dozens of people wrote in with all kinds of questions (one poor guy even asked me for legal advice on how to stop his estranged wife and child moving to the other side of the world without him). The most common predicament by far – 80% ran along these lines – went like this: 'Dear Humfrey, I like someone but I don't know if he/she likes me. What should I do?'

Added together, all the stories I've told in this chapter and all the other times I've seen this situation happen tell me you should tell that person how you feel (unless they're married or have children or both).

My point is this: don't be afraid to take a risk. Sure, it might not work out. You might be left heartbroken if a guy you've liked from afar for years turns you down flat. But isn't that better than not knowing at all? Isn't it better in every possible way to try and then fail than to not try at all?

Hell, yes it is.

Be brave and go for what you want because if it works out and you and this friend go on to have a long and happy life together, that is one hell of a prize. Surely that's worth the risk?

If it doesn't, at least you tried. Don't be one of those people who doesn't have a go because they're scared of failing. That's no way to live, whether in your love life or any other part of your existence.

A word of warning
(final word, part two)

That doesn't mean you should go around declaring your undying love to any guy you're remotely interested in. Remember that doing nothing is also a good tactic. Use your judgement to decide which to employ.

MEN SENSE:

1. Choose the friends that you have flings with very carefully.
2. Don't be mean to your friends.
3. Be honest.
4. Be brave and take risks – the potential rewards are huge.
5. If it doesn't work out, try your best to save your friendship.

Chapter Nine

Why Chasing Your Fantasy
Mr Right Is Wrong

- Why dream men never live up to expectations
- How men portray themselves compared to how they really are
- Why a real man doesn't pretend to be something he's not
- How to spot a fake

When you start reading the next paragraph, you may be under the impression I've forgotten this book is supposed to be about dating. But bear with me because I haven't lost my mind. There is a purpose to this tangent. All will become clear.

When I first started my business about four years ago, an opportunity appeared that seemed extraordinary. Someone was starting a company and he needed my help and in return he would give me a share of his business. If his projections were accurate this share would make me a millionaire several times over in no more than twelve months. At the time I was desperate to get my teeth into some work that might earn me long-term rewards, so I jumped at this chance.

To cut a long and painful story short, I ended up earning absolutely nothing. Literally nothing, not even a penny. In fact I lost money, as did the company, and the whole 'enterprise' failed dismally.

When I first heard about this supposedly amazing opportunity, I was both inexperienced in the business world (I'd never seen something like this before) and desperate for something like this to come into my life. Consequently I jumped into it far too quickly, committing myself totally without doing anywhere near enough analysis of the situation and failing to notice any of the warning signs.

Now transfer the whole scenario from my professional life to my love life. Are you with me so far? I'm talking about human behaviour and specifically how we react at vulnerable moments in our lives.

So how does that relate to Mr Right?

In the same way this business 'opportunity' was sold to me, guys and girls present themselves to people they date as one thing when actually they're something else. The person to whom they're presenting themselves buys into the illusion because this new love interest seems so perfect at that precise moment in their life.

This happens all the time, and if there's one bit of advice I was given after that business failed that can be applied to someone's love life as well as in their professional existence, it's this: if something (or someone) is too good to be true, then it's almost definitely not true.

But – and you must remember this – most people, guys and girls, do not deliberately misrepresent themselves. These are not necessarily purposeful deceptions and there are many more honest and mistaken people in the world than there are emotional conmen and conwomen.

An example follows.

But first, a confession. I'm sorry to have to tell you this but I do get it wrong sometimes. Even with all the experience I have of my own and my friends' lives and stories, I am not right all the time.

I know what you're thinking, if the writer of a book supposed to solve the mysteries of the male mind can't get it right about his fellow men's motivations every time, what hope do you have? None? Well, no, not none. You do have *some* hope. Quite a lot, actually.

But you must accept that where human beings and their emotions are involved, no one can ever be 100% certain of anything. So all I can do is tell you stories, give you my opinion on them and hope you learn from that. The rest is a gamble for which I want to make you as educated as possible.

So, when did I get it wrong? And why is the story relevant?

(One of) the time(s) I got it wrong – OK, there may have been more than one

My friend Chloe was sent by a friend on a blind date with a guy who'd only just broken up with a long-term girlfriend. Chloe decided to ignore this warning sign for several reasons. First, she hadn't had a date in months and second, the friend who set up the date said the guy was definitely nice and also over his ex. Chloe trusted this friend and when she asked me for a man's perspective I said go for it (I knew she hadn't had a date for months and I thought an evening with a guy – any guy – would be good for her).

So Chloe started dating him. The one bit of advice I gave her was to be at least a little bit cautious and not jump in straight away because she has a history of falling for people quickly. 'Find out slowly what kind of person he is and let him get to know you in a non-sexual way,' was the gist of my wise guidance. And in her way she was careful, meaning she didn't sleep with him until the fourth date.

Sleeping with someone on the fourth date is not unwise behaviour, either in general or in this example. Far from it, in fact. In Chloe's case, the guy was attentive, kind, thoughtful and seemed to like her.

But Chloe did make one mistake.

The guy Chloe was dating tried to get her into bed on the second date. This is not necessarily a bad sign. At the time it could have meant he was only interested in sex or, as seemed more likely, simply that he fancied her and couldn't help himself (he's a man, remember). When she said no, Chloe said: 'Not yet. You have to wait until the fourth date for that.' And that second part was her mistake. 'Not yet' is all she should have said. By putting a definite time on when they would have sex for the first time, she gave the game away. From that moment on he knew that if he went on two more dates with her, he would get laid. Whether he was aware of it or not (he might have reacted subconsciously), the mystery and thrill of the chase vanished at that moment even though the sex hadn't even happened yet.

At the time, though, Chloe didn't realise this.

After each of the first three dates, Chloe told me what happened and I agreed that he seemed like a decent guy. He was calling her regularly, being attentive, texting all the time, saying he couldn't wait to see her – all that, even though they hadn't had sex yet. If there was any kind of game going on, it was being played perfectly.

Or so we thought.

After the fourth date, they finally spent the night together and it went brilliantly. They went out on a Thursday night and ended up both taking the next morning off work so they could stay in bed for a few more hours. Chloe was excited and happy and I was both pleased for her and happy at the thought I'd given her the right advice and helped guide her towards something good.

But I was completely and utterly wrong because apart from a few texts over the next couple of days, she never heard from this guy again.

Was this a classic case of a guy hanging around long enough to get what he wanted – sex – and then moving on? At first I thought it was and I cursed him for treating Chloe this way. Typical, sex-obsessed, selfish, uncaring bastard man, she and all her female friends said. I couldn't argue with them because he'd given us all a bad name.

But the truth turned out to be not quite so simple. A few weeks later Chloe looked at his Facebook page (for reasons I don't understand he hadn't de-friended her) and there were photos of him with his ex-girlfriend at a pub lunch on the Sunday three days after his and Chloe's fourth date. And according to his relationship status, that ex wasn't an ex any more. He was back with her.

In hindsight the warning signs were obvious. Chloe was lonely and wanted a boyfriend (I won't say she was desperate for one because that's insulting but she definitely wasn't at a happy stage of her life and she believed a relationship would change that – always dangerous), and the guy had a huge gap in his life left by his recent ex-girlfriend. Chloe dropped into that gap quickly and easily – she wanted to be someone's girlfriend and he wanted someone to play that role for him. His attentiveness combined with her loneliness made them lean on each other in the wrong way (i.e. a relationship way rather than a 'getting to know each other' way) far too early. And when his ex came calling, he realised Chloe had been nothing more than a temporary replacement for her. The ex was the real thing and so he went back to her.

And so it was that my first thought – that it was too soon for him to date someone else – which was also Chloe's initial worry, turned out to be absolutely right.

Remember what I said about instincts? Both our instincts were right in this situation but we both overruled them because he seemed perfect. Big mistake.

Was he a bad boy?

I expect some people would say yes, this guy was a very bad boy but I'm not sure it's quite so clear-cut. This guy didn't deliberately mislead Chloe so I find it hard to judge him harshly. He wasn't malicious or calculating (he wasn't planning to just sleep with her and then move on). Everything he said and did with her was meant sincerely: at the time he thought he really liked her and they were starting something. His motives were undoubtedly good. Ultimately, though, he hurt Chloe anyway and so whether or not he was a bad boy is irrelevant.

But if he *was* a bad boy ...

For the sake of argument, let's say someone who behaves like that *is* a bad boy. By that rationale just about every guy in the world is or is capable of being a bad boy, including me. And if every guy is a bad boy, what's the point of dating any of us when we're all such bastards? There is no point.

So let's not call him a bad boy. Let's instead think that he's a good guy who my friend met at a bad moment in his life – because that's accurate. Finally, while acknowledging that dream men never live up to expectations, let's look for the good in him and the rest of the guys in the world. It is there, just not all the time.

One step closer to the one

At around the same time Chloe's story happened, I heard another tale of disappointment from a girl I know, Catherine. She'd met a guy she liked and had been dating him for a couple of months. They were getting on well but he didn't seem to be making a move to make things any more serious and official between them. Eventually Catherine decided enough was enough and she broke up with him.

I remember exactly what she said – that he 'didn't want to put all his eggs in one basket'. The look on her face at the moment she said that, the sadness, disappointment and hurt pride at not being the right basket, stayed with me, because I thought how in a similar situation with a different girl I could so easily have been the guy who made Catherine feel like that. Now, I wouldn't have done that deliberately, just as I'm sure the guy she was seeing didn't deliberately hurt her, but the result was the same – Catherine was upset.

By the way, I also know very well that girls aren't always the ones who get hurt (plenty of guys have felt like she did) but this book is about the male perspective. And, as a man, I still remember the look on Catherine's face.

Why am I telling sad stories?

I'm telling these stories to make a point. The key question is what could or should Chloe or Catherine have done differently? And the answer is nothing at all.

That, I'm afraid, is the harsh reality. Even though neither person did anything wrong, made any major mistakes or was deliberately selfish or mean, someone got hurt. The fact is dating can be tough, for guys and girls. Disappointments happen.

All I can say is that if it happens to you just remember that the one that has just gone wrong means you're one step closer to the one that will go right.

It also means that next time you'll be a bit more experienced and a bit wiser. But don't ever be cynical or pessimistic because there are good guys out there and you'll find one sooner or later. Be patient and don't give up.

Men are useless, part 1,797,456,999,246 ...

I confessed early in this book that men are useless. The odds are you knew this already but I wanted you to know that I know it too and, more importantly, am not afraid to be open about it.

Here's another example. And it's a cracker.

By the way, I put this story in my newspaper column and pretended it was my own (my editors liked stories to happen to me, not my friends) so I'm delighted to now have the opportunity to put the record straight.

Yes, I've done some stupid things in my time. But I didn't do *this* stupid thing ...

A friend of mine, who I'll call Tom for the sake of this story, bumped into a girl with whom he had a fling at university. Her name was Teresa. Five years on he still thought she was hot, so he suggested they meet for a drink. A quick word about Tom: he's very clever, successful, good-looking and entertaining. In short he's a good guy and definitely not the type to do stupid things.

Or so it would seem.

I'm telling you this story to make the point that all guys, even the ones who are A+ flawless perfection on paper, are capable of acts of monumental and comical idiocy. Which means the ideal, perfect man doesn't exist. He can't because we're all human. Which means we all have flaws and moments of weakness and/or stupidity. Even Tom.

So, fast forward a week from the day they bumped into each other and Tom and Teresa were out for drinks in a south London bar. Tom lived fairly close to where they met but when the evening came he was running behind schedule and, in order to not be late, he had to cycle to the venue. With the help of the two wheels he got there on time and everything was fine.

Actually, everything was more than fine because they had a great evening as it turned out. Teresa was single and the old chemistry was still there. They drank vast amounts and ended up snogging each other's faces off. Later on, Tom suggested they go home together and Teresa invited him back to hers. They walked out of the bar and she hailed a taxi. Teresa's flat was only a ten-minute drive away. All very straightforward.

Well, not quite.

Because that was when Tom's male stupidity gene kicked in. Instead of getting in the cab with Teresa, kissing her all the way home and jumping straight into bed when they got there, Tom decided he couldn't leave his bike outside the pub all night. It was locked up and the area was safe but he still couldn't leave it there. I mean, seriously? What was he thinking?

What he did next defies all logical analysis. The only possible explanation is the aforementioned male stupidity gene.

Tom decided he would take his bicycle with him to Teresa's house. But he didn't know where she lived. So did he put it in the back of the cab? Oh no, thought Tom, that would be silly. His idea was much better. He was going to follow – that's right, *follow* – the cab back to Teresa's flat on his bicycle. Yes, *on his bicycle*.

Can you guess what went wrong? Here's a clue: a taxi is faster than a drunk man on a bicycle.

Teresa got in the cab while Tom scurried off to get his bicycle. He fumbled with the lock and eventually got going. Then he stopped behind the taxi and signalled for it to move off.

Sure enough, less than a minute later Tom had completely lost track of the taxi. It turned one corner with Tom following close behind but around the very next bend there were two taxis in front of him and Tom had no idea which one was Teresa's (it was dark and he was drunk). And then they both sped off anyway so even if he had known it wouldn't have mattered.

But all was not lost – Tom still had his mobile phone with Teresa's number on it.

For this bit, I'll hand over to the man himself. Here's Tom: 'As I cycled gently along, not really going anywhere, I reached into my pocket for the phone. I was about to dial Teresa when I rolled over a bump in the road and began to wobble slightly. Being at the wrong end of a bottle and a half of wine and only having one hand on the handlebars did not help me regain my balance and the wobbles got worse.

'As I was about to topple over I grabbed the handlebar with my other hand, dropping my phone on the road in the process. Finally under control, I turned to find the phone. At that moment, another taxi roared past and its front wheel drove straight over it. My phone was smashed to pieces and Teresa's number was lost.'

So that was it. Tom and Teresa's moment of reignited passion was dead and he cycled home alone in a fog of boozy misery. Yes indeed, men are stupid.

Tom and Teresa – the final word

The next news Tom heard of Teresa was an update through friends about three years later.

She had just married an international rugby player.

Poor Tom.

Humfrey Hunter

Mr Big does not exist

Inspired by Tom's example, this is a message to all those girls out there who are waiting for the real world's Mr Big from *Sex and the City*: stop what you're doing right now because you are wasting your time. That man does not exist. He may be all over our TV screens and in magazines but every one of those images is a fantasy. These men are not real. The idea of the constantly in control, 100% alpha male is a fallacy.

Sorry to disappoint you.

Actually, I'm not sorry. There's an important point lurking behind my criticism of girls who are holding out for Mr Perfect and it is this: girls complain that they're under pressure to be things they can't be and in this day and age, I don't blame them. Everywhere you look is Superwoman – the great mother, amazing wife and stunningly successful career woman all rolled up into one slim, beautiful and perfectly presented female form.

But, like Mr Big, these women don't exist either. I simply do not believe that the perception of these superwomen matches the reality of them. Somewhere along that chain something or someone is being neglected. It might be her husband or her children or, more likely, the woman herself who may not have the time or energy to enjoy the people around her who she loves and who love her or to be the person she wants to be rather than the one she feels she should be. Either way, nothing and nobody is that perfect and so I can easily imagine how those images of Superwoman make life difficult for twenty-first-century girls.

And that's the important point: men also feel that pressure and that unrealistic expectation exists for single men too. Men, single or otherwise, are bombarded with images of male perfection that are completely out of reach to the normal guy. Whether it's a model with a six-pack on a billboard or the love of Carrie Bradshaw's life, we too are confronted with images of what we are not and never will be.

And so the conclusion is this: in the same way the airbrushed vision of feminine perfection does not exist, nor does the 'perfect' man. So if you're single and looking for one, stop it. And if you're dating a chap who you think is this perfect guy, think again because he's not. He might well be a lovely, good, honest man but he's not perfect. No one is. That's not to say there aren't amazing, special people out there. There are lots and you'll find one eventually. But perfection in the Mr Big and Superwoman sense is an illusion. It doesn't exist.

Before you start thinking I'm a pessimist because of all this talk of perfection being a myth, I have one other thing to say: perfect people might not exist but people who are perfect for other people most definitely do. Couples whose qualities and flaws complement each other's, who make the other a stronger and better person and who together become something truly special. So anyone looking for the perfect guy or girl should rethink and instead start looking for the guy or girl who is perfect for them.

Money, money, money, isn't very funny . . .

But that does not stop some people believing the hype about these non-existent über-beings. Very often these imagined people are rich and money is often the trigger for much unhappiness when one person's financial aspirations do not match the bank balance of the person they're in a relationship with.

Here's a friend of mine's experience of how an ex-girlfriend's obsession with money made him miserable: 'When we first got together I was in the early stages of my career so didn't earn much. I work for a magazine, one of those creative and fun businesses where people love their jobs and have a great time but do not earn good cash until they get quite a long way up the ladder.

'So in my early and mid-twenties I would bounce out of bed in the mornings because I was so happy about how I spent my days. I was doing my dream job and professionally could not have been happier. I was incredibly lucky and I knew it. Very few people get to feel like I do about their work. But I wasn't rich.

'When we left university, my ex had started working at an investment bank in their publicity department. She was one of those girls who didn't really have a career plan so just got herself a job, any job which paid her enough to live on. She was bright so it was a good one and she was doing well, which was great.

'The problems between us began because she was immediately surrounded by very, very rich guys and girls who were either on the way to earning big bucks themselves or were there simply because they wanted to bag one of those rich guys for their husband.

'The first sign of real trouble came when during a conversation about where we were going to go for a holiday, I said my finances couldn't stretch to the kind of places her colleagues visited. She replied, "I wish you were a banker." At the time I didn't realise the significance of that comment. I thought it was just one of those things someone says when they're a bit frustrated. I've done it myself.

'But as time went on, more and more things happened. I would occasionally hear from her that banks still took on people of my age (twenty-six or so by then) as trainees, so if I wanted a career change it wasn't too late. But I did not want a career change. I still loved what I did and although I was doing well, I hadn't yet made the big breakthrough to being one of my industry's high earners. I was still young and in my defence (I still get defensive about this now even though it was years ago) very few people do make that breakthrough until they're at least thirty.

'Eventually I realised what was going on with her. I realised she was starting to resent my job and the lack of millions it brought in. She couldn't understand why I loved it so much or why I was very happy to dedicate my life to it. All she was interested in was my pay cheque.

'I remember once I had a big story printed in a very famous magazine – a huge achievement for me and the high point of my career – and when I told her about it, the first thing she asked was how much I had been paid for it. When I told her she sneered and said, "That's nothing to be proud of." To me it was a lot of money but to a banker it was probably no more than a couple of rounds of drinks. And I'd sweated blood over that story.

'I think it was at that moment when something finally clicked in my head, because when she said those words my excitement about my achievement vanished like a burst balloon. Why did she make me feel like that? Despite me being happy doing my job and being good at it, despite me always having good stories to tell her and her friends, she wasn't happy because all she wanted was for me to be rich. I finally realised that, to her, my feelings and ambitions came second.

'Eventually I had enough. She'd asked me once too often how long it would be before my income hit six figures. I felt like she didn't understand me, didn't understand what I was trying to do with my life and, worst of all, didn't care about what I wanted for myself. All that mattered to her was having a rich man to look after her and for her to show off about.

'Being made to feel like I wasn't enough in that way made me desperately unhappy. I felt unsupported, unappreciated and as if what I wanted for myself didn't matter. So in the end I broke up with her, and after I'd done it I did not feel so much as a tinge of regret. Not once.

'Now, a few years on, my career has gone exactly the way I hoped it would. I still love my job as much as I ever did and all that hard work has paid off. After a couple of strokes of luck, mainly to do with meeting the right boss at the right time, I made a name for myself and the rewards have followed.

'Do I want to get in touch with my ex and tell her how well I'm doing and how happy I am? I do slightly, yes. But I won't because the real bonus is I'm now with a girl who actually enhances my life. I would do anything for her and she under-stands what I've been through to get where I am. I also believe with all my heart that she would still love me just as much if it all went horribly wrong tomorrow.

'That is the kind of love I've always wanted.'

The epilogue

His ex wanted Mr Big from *Sex and the City*. What she got was Mr Nice Magazine Guy from London. Despite being a good, clever and ambitious man he wasn't enough for her and she drove him away. In the end I expect she regretted that.

So how does that relate to dream men?

Of course we understand that girls want a comfortable life. We don't want to live in poverty either. But we don't like being treated like a chequebook with a penis. We are more than that.

Too many girls say their dream man has to be rich, as if money is an end in itself in the quest for happiness (I know most girls aren't like this but plenty are). To those girls I say this: I do understand how you feel about financial security, enjoying good things in life and so on, but please don't let money become so important that it obscures your view of other far more life-enhancing aspects of a man's character, like his kindness, sense of humour or imagination.

Besides, do you really want to be bought? If a guy feels he has to impress you by throwing cash around, then I don't believe that's a good way to begin a relationship. How real can whatever is between you be if it's built on the foundation of how much money he's willing to spend on you? And how much respect can he have for you or himself if that's what he feels he has to do to win you?

Humfrey Hunter

The pressure on men

Let me be clear, it is not only women who put men under pressure. We do it to ourselves. Whether it's our competitive instincts or ego to blame I don't know for sure. But the result is some guys drive themselves on and on in the pursuit of material wealth when it's not making them or the people around them – the people who care most – happy.

For example, I have a friend who has a wife he adores, a beautiful baby, a good job and a lovely house. But he's not as happy as he should be. So what's the problem? My friend feels he has to earn on the same scale his father did and provide his wife and children with everything they could possibly want, not just everything they need. His father was a very wealthy man and so this is a tall order. This troubles him and that's not right.

I grew up without a father (he died of cancer when I was very young) and I tell my friend repeatedly that all his wife and baby and any more little ones who arrive in the future will want is for him to be around and love them. No more than that.

The older I've become the more all this has become clear to me because as I see more and more of my friends get married and have children, and as I became a godfather myself (twice, to Noah and Oliver), I have gained a bit more of an understanding of how my father must have felt when he found out he was going to disappear from the lives of his three children (at the time we were only five, four and one). I have begun to understand what he lost as well as what we lost, most recently on my older sister Rachel's wedding day, when my mother, my younger sister Sarah and I walked her down the aisle and I made a speech. He missed so much, on that day and every other day of our lives since he died: the stress, the worry, the laughter, the

208

tears, the relief, the satisfaction, the pride, all of it. As I write this, Noah is four and to me those years have gone in a flash. That puts into perspective the five years my father had with Rachel.

What I'm trying to say is that we men grow up as we get older and we learn. For me, now, my goals and plans for the future are simple: I want a happy family. Anything else is secondary to that.

So, you see, men put themselves under pressure. We want to be good husbands and fathers. We want to be providers and protectors and be emotionally strong (though these days we're allowed to cry sometimes) and never let our families down. We may not be 'perfect' but most of us do try our best and put ourselves under pressure to do the best we can for our future family.

For most men it's a scary prospect but one we look forward to. That's how I feel, anyway. And even single guys think about this.

MEN SENSE:

1. The perfect man doesn't exist.
2. The man who is perfect for you does exist.
3. Money doesn't matter, as long as you're not on the breadline.
4. Men think about the future.
5. Bad boys aren't bad boys forever.

Chapter Ten

Avoiding Bad Boys

- How to stop yourself from being just another notch on a bedpost
- Why taming a bad boy is not impossible
- How to present yourself
- How to treat him

Baffled. Irritated. Confused.

These are only three of the words I'd use to describe my feelings when I hear about girls who can't stay away from bad boys. Add mystified and you're getting the idea – I just don't understand why girls are irresistibly drawn to guys who treat them badly.

Apparently there is straightforward psychology behind this (which, I'm told, also applies to guys who repeatedly let themselves get walked all over by girls) but I'm not a psychologist so I won't get bogged down in how the female mind works. Instead, I'll tell you how the inability to resist bad boys looks from the male perspective.

I know an attractive, bright girl who spent a couple of years going out with a guy who was, in every possible way, a complete muppet. He was unreliable, selfish and had no ambition or intelligence. He was boorish, rude, treated her appallingly badly (including, I suspect, being unfaithful) and yet rated himself very highly. In fact, he seemed to believe he was *the* greatest male catch on the planet. Clearly he was deluded.

Despite having so much going for her, there was something in this girl's mind that made her buy completely into the elevated view that this feeble excuse for a man held about himself. Why that happened, I do not and never will know. I didn't understand it when they were together and I don't understand it now. To help you understand how I felt (and no, I wasn't interested in her myself), let's ask a few questions about this chump.

Was he physically attractive?

No.

Was he kind?

No.

Was he funny?

No.

Was he interesting?

No.

Did her friends like him?

No.

Did *his* friends like him?

No.

Did he enhance her life in any way at all?

No (although maybe he was good in bed – I never asked about that).

So tell me, please, why did she stay with him? Even if he was the greatest lover in history I don't get it. And that's why I chose the words 'baffled' and 'confused' at the start of this chapter.

Lucky, then, that this book is about guys and not girls and all I have to do is accept that some girls are drawn to guys who treat them badly and then for your sake answer these questions: why are bad boys bad? And what can you do about it?

Inside the mind of a bad boy

As part of my research for this book, I asked a carefully selected group of male friends some probing and sometimes difficult questions (men don't like opening up so most questions are difficult for us). I've used many of the replies in different ways at various points already but there was one answer that was so totally honest and well-written that I wanted to print it in full, along with the question that provoked it. The answer came from my friend Dan C who for quite a long period of his life treated girls very, very badly. The question was: *Have you ever treated a girl badly and regretted it?*

This was his answer:

'I think there's a point in every man's life, usually in his mid-twenties, when he inexplicably grows tired of the whole dating thing. Certainly by the time I hit twenty-four, I'd been dumped (countless times), fallen in love (more than once), had good relationships and bad, long and short, dated prudes and dope fiends, and I noticed a sudden change in my behaviour. With each girl I acted more cavalier – or, let's be honest, more reckless.

'I was in the habit of having two girlfriends on the go at this point. And it wasn't glamorous or manly, I'm sorry to report. More like vaguely pathetic and occasionally amusing, as with the kids who snigger at copies of *Viz* in a newsagent. I'd have the girlfriends calling me at the same time, one on my mobile and one on the landline, having simultaneous conversations, and then brag about it to my mates down the pub after football. It took a somewhat embittered man of Sheffield, himself divorced, to point out that, rather than being cool, I was in fact acting like a complete twat.

'However, his sobering assessment failed to correct my ways. I treated girls worse and worse. In clubs, I'd pull a girl, make out with her, then, as the end of the night approached and with it the promise of a little something, I'd whisper in her ear exactly what I thought of her. My words weren't very complimentary. Let's leave it at that.

'Things reached a nadir one night when I went out with a few mates and got chatting to a sweet girl at the bar. She was twenty-one, but had the sort of expression witnessed only on wide-eyed freshers at uni: big eyes, blue as cornflowers, that gazed at the world with fake cynicism. We drank, danced, drank some more. She encouraged us to do tequila shots, which is always a good indicator of where a night's headed – usually with a crash.

'My crash came at six o'clock the next morning when, desperate to be rid of this girl's company, I hauled my sorry self out of bed and called her a minicab. At 6.20 a.m. on a bitterly cold Sunday morning in Brighton, I shook her awake and said her taxi was waiting outside. I was looking forward to a nice lie-in, cooked breakfast, some banter with my friends, and how this poor girl felt about being made to do the walk of shame at such an hour couldn't be further from my mind.

'But as she got dressed, I heard sniffling and she gave me one long, pitiful look. No sign of anger in her face, which I'd been half-expecting and honestly couldn't blame her for. Just this look that felt sorry for *me*. The girl, whose name I couldn't remember, scribbled something on a piece of paper and left it for me beside my PC. I read it after she left without saying goodbye. Or hello.

'"I hope you stop hating yourself before the next girl," she'd written. I was about to share this note with my flatmates when the words clicked in my head. She was right. I'd treated her like crap, really.

'I thought a lot about that short, single line at the time, and have done ever since. It struck a raw nerve, because it was true. I had low self-esteem. I still kind of do, but it was ten times worse back then. And I masked it through a potent combination of binge-drinking and treating women like disposable razors. It was suddenly clear: the reason I hated on the girls I dated, was because I really hated myself.

'Nowadays I try to work a lot harder at being nice. I'm a long, long way from perfect and can still seem put-out, ignorant and even plain rude. But at least I'm conscious of why I behave the way I do. And whenever I see some bloke in the street bad-mouthing his girlfriend, I know instantly what's going on.

'Girls, I think, need to look at how much a man likes himself before taking things further. And they have to look hard, because a man can hide his self-loathing very well. Trust me, I know.'

The roots of Dan C's devilry

When I read this, what most impressed me was Dan C's self-awareness. Not many men can be bothered or are even able to get to know themselves well enough to talk about their personalities with such accuracy and candour. Also, Dan C is a good friend of mine and someone I like and respect, and I found it difficult to imagine him behaving in this way. So how did this decent guy end up being a bad boy? Or, more to the point, how did this bad boy end up becoming a decent guy?

There was a lot going on in Dan C's mind during his bad boy phase. Not long before, he had been hurt and humiliated by girls a couple of times, experiences that made him wary. And at the same time, he wasn't sure where his life was going professionally plus he had a complicated family life, so had all the attendant insecurities and self-doubt to deal with. Those demons are both stomach-churning and dangerous for the person experiencing them and those around him (take it from someone who knows).

The result for Dan C was that he thought little of himself. He wasn't earning much money, he wasn't making his professional dreams come true and he couldn't get the girl he wanted. So he found two outlets for his frustrations: alcohol and girls. And in the process he became, by his own admission, the worst kind of bad boy.

But he's not that boy any more. These days he's trying hard to be nice and will only get involved with a girl if he really likes her. A few years older, wiser and more established, he's becoming a man.

Men are like fine wine – we get better as we mature

Just like Dan C, I went through a time when I was beset by worries about work, where my life was going and what I was doing with it. I worried that I was wasting my time, that I was never going to amount to anything, that I would disappoint everyone who cared about me, that I would never be able to provide for a family and I would end up as a poor, lonely laughing stock. At moments like this I believe a person learns the true meaning of fear and it was without doubt the most stressful period of my life.

To keep my spirits up I used to regularly remind myself of the Baz Luhrmann lyric:

'Don't feel guilty if you don't know what you want to do with your life. The most interesting people I know didn't know at twenty-two what they wanted to do with their lives. Some of the most interesting forty-year-olds I know still don't.'

That and watching *Entourage* (easily the best thing ever to appear on a TV screen) were the keys to keeping my state of mind vaguely positive.

When I was going through this time, I didn't want to get close to anyone. I had friends, both male and female, and without them and my family I honestly don't know where I'd be today. But while my family and friends were more important to me than I could ever express (and still are), I felt like there was no space in my head or my life for romance. I think this was because I didn't want to make myself even more vulnerable than I already was. My future was at risk so why put my heart on the line as well?

I dated girls but I knew nothing serious was going to happen, not because of them but because of how I felt, which was a long way from the happy, relaxed and confident person I wanted to be. I was always honest about my no-commitment approach but I found that even when girls knew there was no possibility of a relationship, they became emotionally involved anyway, which made everything far more complicated than I wanted it to be. Even though I was being honest, I felt guilty about hurting them.

At the time – this was shortly after I turned thirty – I thought of myself as a work in progress and the result was I became someone who could be described as a bad boy. I didn't lie or mislead anyone but I was selfish and emotionally unavailable.

I was growing up, finding out more about myself, and eventually I got to the stage in my early thirties where I felt like I was on the right path. I began to be more confident about what I was doing, happier in myself. A large part of this new satisfaction with life came from my work. Since I left university and work became more about the rest of my life than earning money to pay for the next few months' beers, I have never been good at applying myself to a job simply to earn money because I couldn't dedicate myself to something unless I'm passionate about it.

This has always been a weakness of mine but by this time, thankfully, I felt I'd found my niche doing something I was truly passionate about and I was happier than I'd been for a long time.

Not long after that, I stopped being a bad boy.

Dan C and I learned to love ourselves – how sweet!

All joking aside, I learned through these experiences that there really is something in the old saying about a person having to learn to love themselves before they can love someone else. I'll come back to this later in the book but I mention it now so you realise this kind of mental process happens in guys as well as girls.

The relevance now is this: while it is unquestionably a positive thing for a person to learn to love him or herself, you don't want to get involved with that person until they've reached the end of that learning process. Exactly the same applies to guys and girls.

Bad boy number three – a good guy

Gordon was a nice guy for years and years. He had serious girlfriends and lots of female friends and didn't sleep around. He was a happy guy.

And then things changed.

A couple of relationships went wrong and Gordon felt he got a raw deal from the girls involved. These incidents damaged his confidence and, coupled with his age at the time – twenty-five or so, when he was trying to build his career – they blended in such a way that Gordon became a player. He started sleeping around, having meaningless flings with girls he met in all kinds of places (he's a clever, bright charmer so once he'd switched into his new persona, he was very successful).

In exactly the same way Dan C and I did, Gordon put barriers up and the consequence was no one could get close to him. And his slightly distant-but-nice-guy persona meant any girl he dated started going mad for him – girls can't resist a bad boy, remember.

For these girls, trying to tie Gordon down was like laying siege to the walls of a castle, the castle being Gordon's heart.

Their problem was that Gordon had absolutely no interest in opening up the gates.

You see, this is what a bad boy is – a castle with really strong, high walls and the only way any girl can get in is if someone inside the castle actually decides to open the gates and invite you in. You have very, very little chance of *persuading* someone to open up the castle. The gates will open up eventually but in their own time, and the decision could be conscious or subconscious depending on who lives in the castle.

But you have virtually no hope of making those gates open at the moment you want them to. That's nothing personal – I'm sure you're lovely – it's simply a reflection of how men work. During some periods in our lives, we're unavailable. Doesn't matter who comes knocking at our castle gate. No one's allowed in.

Fact: most bad boys grow out of being bad boys. But you can't force them to do it.

When the gates finally open

Like Dan C, Gordon is clever and funny and growing as a person and when he eventually opens his gates up again, whichever girl is welcomed in is going to be lucky. He will be good to her because he is essentially a good guy.

So for Dan C, Gordon and myself, we have been bad boys at times but really we are good guys and time will prove that – when we're ready to let someone into our castles.

OK, that's enough about castles,

Let's look at the last paragraph of Dan C's story. In it, he advises girls to avoid guys who have low opinions of themselves (by that I mean guys with low self-esteem beyond the usual levels. After all, everyone has insecurities). This is a straightforwardly sensible thing to do.

But how can you tell if a guy falls into this category? If you don't think simply his age is to blame (and if he's still behaving like a bad boy in his late thirties then it's definitely not an age thing), then I believe there are two warning signs to look for in a guy. Watch out if he is either:

1. completely lacking in confidence

or

2. has too much confidence.

A guy who has no confidence should be avoided because he may be a bad boy like Dan C, while a guy who is over-confident is likely to be trying to compensate for something, which means the supreme self-belief is an act. And you don't want to be with an actor.

The bad bad boys

It's not always easy to look at someone and assess their confidence. In fact, sometimes it's impossible. So here's another way. And the guys it applies to include the ones you should avoid always, at all costs.

These are the guys who manipulate girls for fun, who only ever want sex and to know that a girl likes them to boost their own egos, regardless of the emotional collateral. These guys play games to get girls to fall in love with them purely as a challenge, and see women simply as conquests.

Before you panic and decide to stay single forever or become a lesbian, there aren't actually loads of these guys around. But they do exist. And you'll know you've encountered one by the way he treats you.

The warning signs – how to pick out a bad boy

Does he repeatedly blow hot and cold, sometimes ignoring your messages, thus leaving you feeling tense and anxious and constantly thinking about when he's going to get back to you? At other times, does he reply immediately, wanting to see you as soon as possible? If so, then he's a bad boy and he's playing you. I'm talking about being deliberately aloof and distant, ignoring messages from you rather than just not texting you for a day (that's a different type of guy). If a guy is displaying this kind of calculating character then you do not want or need him in your life. He will not bring good things.

Equally, if he starts telling you how great you are but at the same time making it clear he doesn't want a girlfriend, you should treat him as if he's just as toxic. The fallout for you will be the same: you'll end up getting hurt.

What can you do?

It's simple: don't stand for this kind of behaviour because you deserve better. A guy should treat you with respect and if he doesn't, stop playing his games. That means don't see him, don't text or phone him and don't take his calls. Most importantly, though, do not have casual sex with him. You will be nothing but a comfort blanket, albeit a warm, soft, sweet-smelling one.

And remember this: unless he's a total waste of space, a guy who is really into you will treat you with respect.

Bad boys and the bad things they do

If you've ever encountered a bad boy, I hope he wasn't as bad as these five:

Bad Boy 1: He woke up one morning after a big night out, with a sore head and very little memory of what had gone on. He went to his kitchen, where his flatmates were making tea and toast. He was having a chat with them when a girl appeared in the doorway. He introduced himself politely, determined to be well mannered despite his throbbing head. She looked horrified. 'We slept together last night,' were her only words before she grabbed her bag and ran out of the flat.

Bad Boy 2: He went on a blind date with a girl who got spectacularly drunk – so drunk she had to call her flatmate to help her get home. The flatmate needed Bad Boy 2's help to get the drunk girl home. When they got her home, he thought he had nothing to lose so tried his luck with the flatmate. And he got lucky. The next morning as he was sneaking out, drunk blind-date girl came out of her bedroom at exactly the right/wrong time and saw him. 'Where have you been?' she asked. He thought quickly. 'I didn't think it would be right to stay in your bed with you so I slept on the sofa.' Drunk blind date smiled at him, impressed by his chivalrous behaviour. 'How about coming in now?' she asked. An hour later, Bad Boy 2 slunk out of the house trying desperately not to be spotted by the flatmate.

Bad Boy 3: On a holiday with his unsuspecting girlfriend, Bad Boy 3 completely failed to control his wandering eye. Seeing so many other women in bikinis who were out of bounds was too much for him, so one evening he ground up a couple of sleeping pills and dropped them into his girlfriend's food. A couple of hours later she started feeling sleepy. As soon as she conked out, he headed to the nearest bar and start working his magic on one of the girls in there. After an energetic visit to a room in another hotel he made it back to his girlfriend before she even knew he'd gone out. Then he did the same thing the next night. And the one after.

Bad Boy 4: Living with his girlfriend didn't stop Bad Boy 4 from indulging in his two favourite hobbies: keeping fit and sleeping with other girls. He met a girl who lived five minutes' run away from him and when he wanted to spend time with her he would tell his girlfriend he was going for a run for an hour, run for five minutes to the other girl's house, stay there for fifty minutes and then run home again, by which time he would most definitely need a rest.

Bad Boy 5: A few months before Bad Boy 5 and his girlfriend went travelling together, they decided to move in with her parents to help them save money for the trip. Bad Boy 5 started work at lunchtime every day while his girlfriend and her father left the house hours earlier. Her mother, however, didn't work at all, so she and Bad Boy 5 were alone together every morning. They found a way to fill the time.

Another kind of bad boy, or my friend has the cheek to blame me after she gets blown out (it depends whose side you're on)

A female friend sent me an email with a story about a boy she'd met. This is what it said: 'I was on the Tube going to work in the morning and there was a guy in suit (City-type) sitting opposite me. The girl sitting next to him got up to get off and the train jerked and she fell hard into his lap. They were both shocked but he was very sweet to her and reassured her because she was mortified.

'Then a pregnant woman did the exact same thing, got up and fell into his lap, and all the while I was giggling and catching his eye. So, I blurted out something along the lines of "Wow . . . all these women falling into your lap!" and he grinned and said "What can I say?" We then went through an uncomfortable period of smiling at each other.

'When the train stopped at my stop, he held out his hand and helped me up to "ensure I didn't fall". He then walked me out the station and asked if he could . . . wait for it . . . "catch me for drink". We had a drink and a very nice evening and then lots of texting and phone calls from him . . . and then nothing. Like he'd fallen off the face of the Earth.

'I'm guessing he either has five kids in a foreign country, or just isn't that into me, as I haven't heard from him in a couple of weeks. He started off a gentleman and ended up a jerk, as do so many men. Sigh.

'What's funny about the story is that I only said something to him because of one of your columns. So it's actually all your fault.'

Was that really my fault?

Maybe slightly. My friend might not have flirted with this guy quite so much if I hadn't told her the story of my failed chat-up line on the Tube (you may remember that from Chapter One). So I'll take some responsibility for her behaviour.

What's really interesting is my friend's interpretation of *his* behaviour because her analysis is absolutely spot-on. Either he changed his mind about whether or not he liked her or he was already involved with someone else (more likely he had a girlfriend rather than five kids in a foreign country).

The second explanation, that he had a girlfriend, was far, far more likely to be true. After a good first date, the main reason for a guy not arranging a second is that there's someone else in the background.

So my bet is that he met my friend at a moment when he was having some doubts about his relationship. He would have been swept along by the romance of their meeting. The way she, an attractive girl, made her interest in him so obvious would have flattered him. So he decided to meet up with her.

As for the date itself, I expect he had a good time, but when it came to the end of the evening and the right moment for him to kiss my friend, he decided not to let the flirtation go any further.

He was a jerk for going out on a date with my friend in the first place, sure, but he deserves some credit for not actually pushing the situation as far as a full-on affair.

But what about my friend? Should he have called and told her what the problem was? Probably. But the easiest option (and men like easy options) was to cut off all contact. I expect he even deleted her number because she really never did hear from him again.

Does that make him a bad person?

It doesn't make him a particularly good person but if my interpretation of what went on is accurate then he could have been much, much worse. If that's the definition of a jerk, then he's a jerk.

Now, I don't consider myself a jerk, but I know there have been times when I've been guilty of jerk-like behaviour and the truth is just about all men, if they're being honest, could name at least one occasion when they've acted a little dubiously. For example, not long after my friend Robbie came out of a relationship he dated a girl called Rona for a short while. They went out three or four times before he decided that, nice though Rona was, he didn't fancy her. So he stopped contacting her.

Does that make him a coward? Maybe. But a jerk? Possibly not because he made sure he stopped calling her before things got too serious, in other words before they slept together.

'Typical male coward,' I hear you cry anyway. But, it's not quite that simple. If after four dates he'd said to Rona, 'This should end because I don't fancy you,' wouldn't that have been a bit cruel? I think so. Less cowardly, yes, but still cruel. At the time he decided he'd rather be a coward than cruel. And in his defence, don't forget he could have slept with her but didn't.

Anyway, about two months later, Rona rang him to have a go at him for the way things ended. During their conversation, she asked Robbie why he stopped calling and texting her. He didn't say anything because, as before, he didn't want to be cruel to her.

Then she offered him an easy way out. 'You weren't ready for another relationship, were you?'

'No,' he replied, relieved. 'I wasn't ready. And I'm sorry for my bad behaviour.'

'That's OK, I understand,' Rona said. 'But you should have told me at the time.'

At the end of the call she was happy, even though Robbie had lied. So does that make Robbie a jerk and a coward? He stopped calling her and then lied about why so yes, I suppose it does. But like the guy who met my friend on the train, Robbie could have behaved much, much worse.

And weirdly, if he had lied *earlier* by telling Rona they were breaking up because he wasn't ready for another relationship instead of simply stopping calling her, he'd have actually been doing the right thing. So really, his only sin was lying too late. Which is an odd kind of logic, but one which makes sense here.

Taming your bad boy is not impossible

Not impossible, but very, very difficult. It requires cold-hearted patience and the ability to deny yourself something you really want – time with him. And, of course, luck, because your campaign has to coincide with him voluntarily leaving his bad boy phase.

So, if you feel you're falling under a bad boy's spell (and the chances are if you're worrying about it, it's happening), then pull away sharpish. Don't hang around just in case your instincts are wrong. Trust your instincts – they are your subconscious assessing the available evidence in the blink of an eye and then transmitting its conclusions to you in the form of an impulse. That's what your instincts are, the sum total of the knowledge and rationality you've developed through your life. So listen to them. They're more powerful than you think (and if you don't believe me, read *Blink* by Malcolm Gladwell).

Anyway, back to bad boys. As I was saying, trust your instincts. If they say beware, start playing it cool. Make him do all the running, all the arranging to meet up, and do not let things progress beyond friendship until your instincts tell you he's ready. This may take months and it may well never happen. But it's your only chance of taming a bad boy. Go back to basics. Deny him what he wants (which is easy access to you), because denying him something is the only way to convince a man of its value.

That's not to say you shouldn't be friendly and fun and nice to him. But don't let yourself fall into a semi-relationship. You want to know this guy when he's over his bad boy phase, not while he's in the middle of it. And do not, whatever you do, allow yourself to have any faith whatsoever in him. Because the overwhelming probability is that a bad boy will let you down.

The Golden Rule

This is the Golden Rule for dealing with bad boys, whether they're the soon-to-grow-out-of-it kind or the player-to-his-bones kind: if he doesn't commit to you, then treat him like he's a bad boy. Get him out of your life. And if you can't go that far just get him out of your bed.

Once a doormat, always a doormat (in his mind, anyway)

I've already told you how the same guy can be completely different from one week to the next (i.e. a bad boy with one girl and then good with the next, once he's turned over a new leaf).

But there is something I haven't told you about bad boys: if a guy starts off treating you badly, it's highly unlikely, nigh on impossible, that he'll ever think of you as anything other than someone he can treat badly. So nothing significant will ever happen between you. You'll never get a second chance. I know that sounds harsh but it's me being honest. The fact is, if you've let a bad boy walk all over you for a while and then you pull away from him, hoping that one day he'll come back to you and be the perfect boyfriend, you need to think again. It's not going to happen.

I'm sorry if that shatters some dreams but that's the way it is. Once that mystique has gone from a girl, it never comes back. Not in my experience, anyway. And give me a second to think if I know anyone it has happened to . . .

No, nothing. I can't think of anyone.

Back to the same old story

Once again we come back to the same old principles. There is only one way to get a bad boy to change his ways and be good to you: don't rush in. That means get to know him as a friend and don't have sex with him unless he's really convinced you he's ready for a proper relationship. If all he wants is sex and no commitment then you should stay away. So don't be there when he wants you. Play it ultra-cool – don't be cold to him but don't be there for him whenever and however he wants. Don't answer booty calls. Don't be one of the girls who is a friend-with-benefits, because you can be sure you're not the only one.

Of course, if all you want yourself from your bad boy is casual sex, then answer booty calls as often as you want and have a great time. There's nothing wrong with doing this. But it will reduce even further the already tiny chances of this bad boy becoming your boyfriend.

Men have feelings too

Friendships with bad boys are funny things. As you know, bad boys aren't always bad people. A bad boy is often a good guy who is going through a phase, which means you'll easily become platonic friends with him. But you need to be careful here if you want to develop a romantic relationship with him, because if he starts talking about the issues he has – the ones that stop him from wanting to get into a relationship – you're putting yourself in the wrong role in his mind. Don't be the person he confides in, the friend who helps him through this difficult time. If you are the girl who listens to him and makes him feel better (which should *not* include sleeping with him occasionally), you are unlikely to be the girl he ends up with. He will associate you with that period of his life, the transition rather than the conclusion.

If you can feel this happening with a guy you're really

interested in, pull away from him. Don't let yourself be dragged into this kind of pseudo-romance.

B

I can't let a chapter about bad boys go by without talking about B. He is the stereotypical bad boy. He is constantly on the lookout for girls he can date. He'll meet them, date them, sleep with them once or twice and then move on. People used to be amused by the way he behaved (example: he once went to the STI clinic to get tested and then pulled at the bus stop on his way home), but the longer it goes on, the less funny it becomes, for his sake as well as the girls he meets. However, I do believe that sooner or later he'll grow out of it because B is a guy just like any other.

In fact, I'm going to tell you my theory about B. He is rampantly insecure and goes around pulling lots of girls not simply to entertain himself (although that is part of it) but really just to prove he can. I put this theory to him once. His response? 'You're probably right but I don't care. I'm happy.'

The guy you *do* want

You want a guy who can't help getting in touch with you. A guy who wants to talk to you all the time and see you whenever he can. A guy who would never dream of being deliberately aloof and distant because he wants you to know exactly how he feels about you. He wants you to be sure of his feelings for you because he wants you to feel secure and safe enough to let yourself feel the same about him. A guy who wants to be good to you because of how you make him feel about life: happy, positive and optimistic. A guy who will love you in the way you want to be loved. This is the guy you want and they do exist.

I know this because despite my cynicism and occasional bad boy behaviour, I became one.

Why don't nice guys get the girl? Why not? Come on, tell me! Why not?

Just about the worst reason a girl can give a guy for not being interested in him is that he's 'too nice' for her. Look at it from our point of view: we meet a girl we like and precisely because we like her we decide to do everything properly, which means calling her regularly, deliberately noticing and complimenting her shoes and her hair and even listening to what she says – exactly what all women say they want.

This means abandoning our default patterns of behaviour, such as ignoring her for the occasional fortnight, making drunken booty calls and maintaining we can still pull other girls under the thin pretext that we 'haven't had the relationship chat yet'. This is no way to treat a girl on whom we are genuinely keen. So when a special girl does come along, we don't do it. Instead, we are nice.

But does this approach help us get the girl we want?

The hell it does.

Example: a friend of mine, Steph, started seeing a clever, good-looking guy who seemed like a gentleman at a time when she wanted a boyfriend. Perfect? Not quite. By the fourth date he was doing all that nice stuff described above and more, calling when he said he would and proactively arranging dates. In short, he was playing no games whatsoever. He liked her and he was letting her know he did. But suddenly she thought he was getting a bit too familiar and a bit too thoughtful and instead of seeing him as an honest, good-natured guy, in Steph's eyes he became a stifling wet blanket.

The final straw came when he went on a stag weekend to Prague and began texting her about how beautiful the architecture was and how spectacular the bridges were. This did not go down well. Steph told me she'd have preferred it if he'd sent her pictures of Czech strippers and told her how great their lapdancing moves were.

Apparently this would have given him 'edge' and made her fancy him.

Sorry, Steph, but that's just bonkers. What was he supposed to do? Deliberately treat you badly to make you like him? Why, I asked, do you want him to do that? Her answer left me furious on his behalf. 'If something is that easy to get, it's not worth having,' she said. With a straight face. Countless relationships must have fallen by the wayside for pathetic reasons like this. Or maybe he's being the male equivalent of the roadkill moose. There's a thought.

Anyway, girls, please stop saying one thing and doing another. Don't say you want to be treated properly and then complain when you are. Give the nice guys a chance. It's you who are missing out.

But bad boys fall in love too. And when they do, they fall just as hard as everyone else. As I did when after a long period of not being interested in or ready for something serious, one day I met someone who changed my outlook completely.

Does bad boys' bad behaviour mean they miss out on Miss Right?

I don't think so. There's no 'one that got away' for me. I don't look back on my recent single years and wish I'd had anything more serious with any other girl I've ever met.

To be completely honest, the one regret I have about my love life since I discovered girls as a nervous teenager is that I didn't have a long-term girlfriend, as in someone I was with for a year or two, until I met Girlfriend X towards the end of my university days. Looking back, I wish I had because those relationships can be brilliant and make for great, happy memories. But for whatever reason – my own fault, I expect – I never got beyond about three months.

For B, however, I think there is a one that got away – his very first girlfriend. They broke up before they went off to university, where he expected to find worlds of girls like his ex. I've never met her but according to him she was as sweet and beautiful as it's possible for a girl to be. He's been looking for someone as lovely as her ever since. Interesting.

This whole chapter summed up in one line

If you think you're going to end up as just another notch on his bedpost, don't let yourself become a notch at all.

MEN SENSE:
1. If a man is unreliable, he is to all intents and purposes a bad boy.
2. If you suspect someone is a bad boy, be cautious.
3. Bad boys aren't bad forever.
4. If a boy is bad to you, don't tolerate it.
5. Bad boys can make good friends.

Chapter Eleven

Keeping His History in the Past and Glossing Over Yours

- Why a man with a past isn't always someone to be avoided
- Why he doesn't want to know about your past but can't help asking – the sore tooth approach
- What you should and shouldn't tell him
- How to stop both your pasts from affecting the present and future

Some men are completely secure and never bat an eyelid about their girl's past. These are guys who either know absolutely everything and don't care (and usually laugh about it) or guys who don't ask because nothing that happened before they met her matters at all. These are the cool, calm and collected chaps who live at one end of the spectrum.

Way over at the other end are the guys who obsess constantly over who and what she did before their relationship started, torturing themselves with images of their beloved in states of ecstatic contortion with other men. This obsession makes men feel jealous and threatened and the consequences are unpleasant for both the man in question and the girl he's involved with.

Luckily, most guys land somewhere in the middle. Most of the time our girl's past doesn't bother us but occasionally it does. These feelings will be triggered by any number of things that make us feel insecure and unhappy, things that aren't necessarily to do with our girlfriend.

This all goes back to us seeing our girl as a thing of great value, which means we hate the idea that other guys had any kind of intimate encounter – however meaningless or not – with this girl we think so much of. At times we might feel jealous and insecure and threatened. Guys a bit further up the jealousy scale will wonder what type of sex she had with these guys, torturing themselves with the details in the process. If she had wild times, did she love those wild times more than she loves being with a boyfriend?

This, then, leads to the insecure man wondering if the relationship sex he's having with this girl is really satisfying for her. And how is she going to feel when they've been together for a while and are having that nice, intimate couple sex? Will he be enough for her? Were those guys better in bed than he is? Does she think their sex life is boring? Does she wish she was with someone else?

This is obviously a worst-case scenario (frankly it's one step away from insanity) and very few guys think like this unless they're drunk and feeling self-pityingly emotional (i.e. pathetic). In fact most of us know this kind of thinking is utterly pointless and we understand we're being stupid because if she's with us now it's because she wants to be. Plus, everyone has a past and whatever happened in that past is what makes her the girl we love today. So who cares, right? Most of the time, that's how we think.

This is an important point about male jealousy and insecurity so pay attention: a guy's insecurities are not predicated on how many people you've slept with. A guy will be as insecure and jealous of four past lovers as he will be of four hundred. The very fact you've slept with and cared about other guys is what matters.

So if you have a colourful past and your man kicks up a fuss about it, don't beat yourself up or start regretting what you've done because how he feels is *not your fault*. What matters is what you do after you meet him, not before, which he should understand. If you care about the guy and he's even slightly upset about your past, simply make him feel better. Tell him it's him you're with now, you love him, everything's better now you're with him, you're happy and don't want to go back to the days when you used to take on whole rugby teams (if that's what you did). Reassure him. In a nutshell, treat him how you'd like him to treat you if you were in his shoes and feeling how he's feeling.

What's going on in his head

We all know girls have had lovers before us (we're not stupid) and how that relates to our view of the 'ideal' girl is hard to compute. On the one hand, the thought of your girlfriend – or a girl a guy wants to be his girlfriend – sleeping with someone else is horrible even when it happened before you met. But on the other hand, no guy wants to go out with a virgin. In fact, if a girl is experienced and interested in the sexual side of life then that is very attractive, not least because the new guy is more likely to reap the benefits of her appetite as well as what she's learned. So it's difficult for us because those are very contradictory feelings – wanting both a virgin and a sex goddess rolled into one female form – and they exist next to each other in our little minds.

On balance, though, we'll take the experienced girl every time.

Sometimes we do judge

But, I'm afraid to say, sometimes we do judge girls by what they've done in their pasts. Not often, though. I can only think of two examples, one of which happened to me.

The one that didn't happen to me

My friend Bill met a girl and he liked her a lot very quickly. They 'clicked' in all the right ways and after a few weeks he was very happy and excited about what was going on. Bill had a feeling something big might be starting.

Then one night he was telling a friend of his about this girl. His friend asked Bill what this girl's name was.

Bill told his friend her name.

Bill's friend went quiet.

Bill asked his friend what the matter was.

Bill's friend said it didn't matter.

Bill said it obviously did matter. So, for the second time, what was the matter?

Bill's friend said it *shouldn't* matter.

Bill said he'd be the judge of what did or didn't matter, let alone what should or shouldn't matter. For the third time, what was the matter?

Bill's friend took a deep breath and told Bill what the matter was: two of their male friends had had a threesome with this girl a couple of years previously.

But, Bill's friend said, that shouldn't matter.

Bill disagreed. It did matter.

And Bill broke up with her.

I felt very, very sorry for Bill because this situation was a nightmare for him. Lady Luck really kicked him in the balls that day. He told me how much he liked this girl but he couldn't look at her without picturing her with his two mates. To be clear, he didn't judge her for having had the threesome, he just didn't want to be with a girl who, every time he looked at her, caused images of her at it with two of his mates to pop into his head.

If Bill had found out a few months later, when he was totally in love with this girl rather than in the process of falling for her, then the result might have been different. He might have thought what he had – a relationship with a girl he loved – was more important than a random naughty night she had a few years back. In my opinion, knowing Bill as I do, this is what would have happened. But because he found out so early on in their relationship, such as it was, the revelation was enough to kill whatever they had stone dead. Which was a great shame.

In Bill's words: 'What could I do? How was I supposed to get round something like that? How could I forget what she'd done? I know she didn't cheat on me so there was nothing I needed to forgive her for but I still felt angry with her, even though I knew it wasn't fair. I hated her for it and I hated my mates for it too.

Then I hated myself for hating them when none of them had actually done anything wrong.

'But I still couldn't bring myself to carry on seeing her. How are you meant to feel in a situation like that? I wouldn't have liked knowing she'd done that with two guys at all but I could have dealt with it because she was single and how could I be angry with her for something she did before she met me? I'd be an idiot to hold something like that against her.

'But knowing it was with two of my friends was completely different. Imagine how I'd have felt if I was out with them all one night? Or how I'd have felt at my birthday party when all three of them were there? Or what if we ended up getting married? I couldn't do it.'

It's very, very hard to say what I would have done in Bill's place. Much as I like to think I'm a liberal, twenty-first century man who doesn't judge people, if I found out that a girl I had just started seeing had had a threesome with two of my close mates a few years before I don't think I'd be able to get past that, simply because, like Bill, I'd think about that every time I saw her.

If I didn't know the two guys it would be different. Sure, I wouldn't be too happy about it (the insecurity would be my issue, not hers) but it wouldn't be enough for me to dump her.

But with two of my mates, well, that's a different story. Although if I was in love with her, I like to think I wouldn't want to let her go for something so irrelevant to what was going on between us.

Anyway, I'll stop speculating because it's guesswork. The fact is I have never heard of another situation like this one happening to anyone else. It was bad luck on both Bill and the girl involved. To be honest, I feel especially sorry for her. What did she do wrong? Nothing. All she did was act a bit wild one night. That's all. And yet she lost a potentially great relationship. Sometimes life isn't fair.

The one that did happen to me

Way back when I'd been single for only a few months, female friends started trying to set me up with single friends of theirs. At the time I was one of the few single guys of that age (thirty) and they wanted to see me happily with a girlfriend. I appreciated their good intentions but after a while I did start feeling like something of a charity case (when you're one of the few single people around, all anyone wants to talk about is your love life, or lack of one). The story for here, though, is about a set-up that didn't even get as far as me meeting the girl involved.

Pause for a couple of quick tips on setting people up

1. If you're trying to set up a female friend with a guy you know, don't *ever* describe her to him as 'pear-shaped and sensible'. This is how one girl was described to me. We never met.
2. If a guy asks to see a photo of the girl he's being set up with, don't shout at him for being superficial and then refuse to let him meet the girl. That is ridiculous behaviour. This also happened to me. Of course we want to know what she looks like. Wouldn't you?

Back to the failed set-up story

A female friend (it's almost always girls who try to set up their friends, male and female) told me about someone she knew who would be 'perfect' for me.

That's big talk, I thought, and big talk doesn't usually lead to anything. But I'm listening.

This girl was apparently great fun, hot, clever and so on, as they all are when being described by every setter-up except the one who said the words 'pear-shaped and sensible'.

But, she said, this one was also 'a bit wild'.

Mmm, that's unusual, I thought, and interesting too because most of the time people bill their friends as perfect wife material rather than 'a bit wild'.

'Really,' I said. 'Tell me more.'

She goes out a lot, I was told.

Good.

She's very loud.

Good again.

She's very bright.

More good.

She's very funny.

Yet more good.

This was very promising indeed. Finally, a photo was emailed to me and that clinched it – I definitely wanted to meet this girl. Maybe being set up wasn't such a bad idea after all.

But then this message came through on email, almost as an afterthought: 'Oh, and a few months ago she went backstage at a [insert name of a famous American rapper which can't be printed for legal reasons] gig and gave him a blowjob.'

What? You're trying to set me up with her and you tell me *that*? Are you stupid?

'I thought guys liked that kind of thing,' replied my friend, 'You know, a bit wild and all that.'

Some kinds of wild we do like. But not that one.

Instead of attracting me, that revelation set my interest in this girl plummeting like an anvil lobbed over the edge of a cliff. Administering sexual favours to rappers might be her idea of a good night out and morally I can't really judge her because if I was as famous as this chap and single I'm pretty sure I would merrily have had legions of girls trooping in and out of my tour bus every single day.

But I'm not him and this bit of knowledge was a huge turn-off. Did I want to be set up with a girl who, as the tabloids would say, performed a sex act on this rapper?

No.

Like Bill and his friends' threesome, every time I saw her I would be thinking of this guy. And this would start at our *first meeting*.

Could anything develop between us from there?

No.

But if your own sexual history makes for a long and interesting read, don't worry, These stories mean that men will only judge a girl for what she's done in her past if the circumstances are exceptional. If you don't believe me, here is what a friend of mine said about his girlfriend and her fruity past: 'Sometimes I get jealous,' he says, 'but I think that happens to everyone from time to time and I'm not going to let the past of the girl I love affect my life now because it has nothing to do with us and nothing to do with me.

'So she was a bit wild for a while, so what? We have a brilliant relationship now. I trust her completely and I want to spend the rest of my life with her. The person she is today is the person I love and her past made her become that person. Of course, her wild antics aren't my favourite topic of conversation but I would never let something like that – something irrelevant to my life – affect my happiness or my relationship with her. Those nights were fun, I'm sure they were, but what we have means something. Our future is much more important than what happened before we met.'

Funnily enough, his past was very, very tame in comparison to hers.

And it works both ways, too. I know a girl whose sister started going out with a guy who told her quite openly that he had slept with ninety women before her, sometimes one at a time, sometimes two and sometimes even three. This bothered her a little at the start. But she seemed far less concerned about it when they got married three years later.

So there is no reason at all to think that anything you have done in the past will affect what you have in the present or may have in the future.

But that is not a free pass to sleep around because I don't think sleeping around in anything other than moderation makes anyone happy, male or female. I think people use regular casual sex as a substitute for affection when they're unhappy, drunk or lonely, or a bit of all three.

The big question: what should you tell him?

To me, this is a simple one. Call me idealistic but if someone you're romantically involved with in a serious way asks you a question, you should answer honestly. Tell the truth. I know there are all those phrases about the truth never hurting the teller and so on, but I don't believe couples should lie to each other. Sure, both people might hear things they don't like, but that's not the point. Honesty between a couple is far more important than a bit of temporary upset about how many people your boyfriend or girlfriend has slept with. Frankly, if anyone involved with someone else can't handle the truth about their past then that's their problem (and I say that as a self-confessed jealous guy). And if there's anything you don't want to know, don't ask the question.

I heard someone say once that no guy wants to be anything more than a girl's tenth lover so girls should lie about how many men they've 'known'. Rubbish, I say. Just tell the truth. No guy in his right mind will reject a girl who's amazing in every other way simply because she slept with too many people before they met. And if a guy does reject a girl for that reason, then he doesn't deserve her anyway.

This, then, is the rule: when in doubt, tell the truth.

Here's another story on a similar subject. A girl, Rebecca, meets a guy, Mr Right, through work. He asks her out and they start dating. A couple of months later, when things are going very well, she's at his house one day and sees a photo of him with one of his friends. She thinks she recognises the friend. She asks after the friend. She discovers she does indeed recognise the friend – they dated a couple of years earlier. His name is Mr Wrong.

Mr Right noticed the look on Rebecca's face when she heard Mr Wrong's name. He knew something was up and, being human, he couldn't help asking if Rebecca knew Mr Wrong. Rebecca told him the truth – that she and Mr Wrong saw each other for about six months and it ended about eighteen months before she met Mr Right.

Mr Right was gutted because Mr Wrong was his oldest friend. They had grown up together. And Rebecca was gutted too. Not only had she upset Mr Right, the best, nicest man she'd met in a long time, but it turned out Mr Wrong hadn't even mentioned her to Mr Right. Despite them being friends since they were nippers, Rebecca wasn't important enough to Mr Wrong to even merit as much as a conversation with his oldest friend, even after six months' dating. Mr Wrong was, as you may have guessed, a player. I feel for Rebecca because her pride must have taken quite a kicking. I can't excuse Mr Wrong's behaviour. That's just what some men do when they're happy being single and don't want any commitment. He would have thought whatever was going on with Rebecca was not important in the wider scheme of things and so didn't even bother mentioning it to his best mate. No excuses. That's just how some men are. (Note: if you've been seeing a guy for six months and haven't even met his best friend, alarm bells should be ringing.)

How did Mr Right feel when he found out that Mr Wrong knew his Rebecca, the girl he had fallen in love with, in ways he hoped his best friend never would?

Absolutely, indescribably horrible is how he felt. Not only would he have to live with the knowledge that Rebecca slept with his best friend (although with no cheating or trust issues involved), but also she was clearly so insignificant in Mr Wrong's eyes that Mr Right was never even told about her. To Mr Right, Rebecca was the girl he wanted to spend the rest of his life with. To Mr Wrong, she was a casual fling. That must have felt hideous and as a fellow man, I feel very, very sorry for him.

So what happened to Rebecca and Mr Right?

This is my favourite part of the story. Mr Right turned out to be a special guy. He was strong and principled and very quickly realised that in Rebecca he'd found a truly special girl and no amount of battering to his ego (from the knowledge that she'd been with his best mate) made any difference to that. If anything, he loved her even more for having had to think through what they had together.

At some stage he would have asked himself if he could stay with Rebecca and thus at the same time he would have contemplated what it would be like to not be with her. It sounded to me as though roughly a nanosecond later he realised that of course he could stay with Rebecca. And not only *could* he stay with her but he should do absolutely anything to make sure he stayed with her because they had something wonderful together. What had happened between her and Mr Wrong long before they met was utterly inconsequential.

A story that still shocks me

I don't think anyone should have to forgive someone for their past, for something that happened before two people met or got together. But if someone I loved cheated on me then like most people I don't think I'd be able to get over it. Which is why this following story left me open-mouthed when I heard it. And still does now. Frankly this story is so, well, odd, that I have to share it. It's about a person's past, it's about infidelity and it's about forgiveness in the most unlikely of circumstances.

That's enough build-up, here's the story.

The story

Sharon and Shaun got together when they were about twenty-seven. Two years later, Sharon suspected Shaun had cheated on her and confronted him. Shaun confessed that yes, he had cheated on her. More than once. It turned out he had slept with about six other girls at regular intervals throughout their relationship. Sharon was understandably distraught.

So, was that the end for this couple?

Nearly.

Sharon, for reasons that make no sense whatsoever to me, gave Shaun two options. The first one was that they break up then and there. The second was for Shaun to go and see Sharon's father and tell him exactly what he had told Sharon. That is to say, he had to confess his infidelities to the father of the girl he'd been cheating on.

That's creative, I thought. And quite a good punishment. I'm impressed. But surely Shaun wouldn't do that? How much humiliation would he want to take to keep a girl he cared for so little he'd slept with six others? Not any, I'd guess.

Wrong.

Shaun did it.

He phoned Sharon's father and said he wanted to see him, drove out to her parents' house, sat down and spilled the story. Now, if I was Sharon's father I think I might have expected a rather different conversation after my daughter's boyfriend of two years asked for a one-to-one chat. One about a marriage proposal, to be exact. I would not in a million years have thought I'd hear that same young man confess to doing the dirty on my offspring. Six times. Frankly I'm surprised Sharon's father didn't reach for a shotgun.

But Sharon's father listened and managed to not attack Shaun (I'm impressed). A few years down the line, Sharon and Shaun are now married and as far as anyone knows, he's been faithful ever since.

In these times of ubiquitous celeb infidelity, this is a hot topic. I have no idea how Sharon managed to get past Shaun's indiscretions. For a guy, I'm not sure it would be possible. If my girlfriend told me she'd slept with six other men over the past two years I cannot imagine being able to feel the same way about her ever again and I do not think I'd be the only one. Sharon,I expect, is the one in a thousand who thinks differently.

To be honest, I can't understand why either of them did what they did. As in, why the hell didn't they just break up? But I've never been in that situation, thankfully, and I hope I never will be.

Me and jealousy, or being jealous of people who are jealous (at least they can be jealous)

For me, by the time I'd been single for two years, I found myself thinking how nice it would be to have someone to get jealous of. It was New Year's Eve and I was seeing it in alone. Worst of all, being single seemed to have become my defining feature thanks to my weekly exposure in my column.

By New Year's Eve, I'd been single for nearly two years and I was a little bit bored of it all (I'd planned for a year, remember). And, to be completely honest, I was beginning to feel a bit lonely. Pretty well all my friends were in relationships and I was getting tired of being asked what was going on in my love life.

I know that makes me sound ungrateful (people only asked because they cared and wanted me to be happy and I was very lucky to have the column), but I did sometimes feel like that's all there was to me. I was Humfrey the Single Guy.

And then I'd remind myself that not only had it been my choice to be single but I was also now writing a column effectively celebrating my single life so I had absolutely no one else to blame for the subject preoccupying people I spoke to. It was all my own fault.

But back to that single life. Much more fun.

New year, new attitude

On that NYE, I decided to think positively. To me, the change from one year to the next would represent a new chapter opening, one I would treat differently to the rest. Optimism was the key, along with the belief that somewhere out there in the world was the right girl for me and it was simply a matter of time before I found her.

But there was one thing I needed to be very careful to avoid: settling.

Why single men are like taxis

My younger sister Sarah has a theory about single men being like taxis who cannot control their lights. A girl who likes the look of one of these taxis is like a passenger, standing at the side of the road waving her hand as it passes by. Sometimes the taxi's light is on and sometimes it is off, which means sometimes the taxi is available and sometimes it isn't. But – and this bit's important – there doesn't need to be someone else already in the taxi for it to not want to stop.

What this means is that if a single man's light is on, then he is liable to get together in a serious way with the next girl he meets who he really likes. If his light is off, however, there is absolutely nothing in the world any girl can do to make him start something serious with her. He is unavailable. Full stop.

I could tell Sarah was on to something because I was no longer thinking like a man whose light was off. I now looked at girls and thought, 'Can I see myself with her?' Even though the answer at this stage was always no, I still had to be careful because I didn't want to be one of those guys who settled, one of those guys who reaches a point in his single life where he wants a girlfriend and the next available girl he meets becomes The One. That is a guy who has settled and I did not want to be one of those.

New Year's Eve, part two

To recap, it was New Year's Eve and I was feeling positive about the world and I wasn't just looking for short-term flings any more.

But I didn't have particularly high hopes of pulling that night because the only NYE I'd had as a single man in the past decade was twelve months previously and a total non-event. The one available girl at the party inexplicably started crying at 9 p.m. and left an hour later with her eyes still streaming. And no, it wasn't my fault. We hadn't even exchanged a word.

Here's how I did on my second single New Year's Eve.

On the night, I went to a pub with my cousin Max and his wife Mareike. It was great fun with lots of booze, cheesy dancing and a few nice-looking girls around. But one stood out – she had short dark hair, wore a slinky purple dress and, through my boozed-up, emotionally vulnerable eyes, looked quite appealing.

It was their local pub so Max and Mareike knew a few people and Mareike asked me if I wanted to be introduced to anyone. I said the girl in the purple dress was the only one I was interested in and because there had been some flirtatious dancing and eye contact going on I thought I might be in with a shot. No chance, said Mareike, she's a lesbian. That wasn't what I wanted to hear but I was having a great night so didn't mind having no girl to chat up.

After the pub, I ended up staying on Max and Mareike's sofa and the next morning she asked me why I hadn't tried anything with the girl in the purple dress. I laughed at this.

'Because she's a lesbian, of course,' I said.

'What are you talking about?' she said.

'You told me she was a lesbian so I left her alone,' I replied.

Mareike looked confused. 'But I didn't say that. I said I thought she liked you.'

What had happened was obvious: my stupid drunken ears destroyed any chance I had with the girl in the purple dress by hearing 'She likes you' as 'She's a lesbian'. I felt like an idiot, which made my hangover even worse.

Later I told B the story. He called me an idiot and said I couldn't pull in a brothel, which was not exactly what I wanted to hear. He also bet me that I wouldn't put the story in my column complete with the name of the pub and, in a last desperate (yes, it was desperate, I admit that, but I also hate losing bets) attempt to rescue the situation, a request for the girl in the purple dress to get in touch.

Well, B lost that bet and I did put the story in my column, complete with an invitation to the girl in the purple dress to contact me. Why did I do it? To shut B up as much as anything else.

Did I hear anything from her?

No.

And, of course, I had to put that failure in the column as well so a few days later 600,000 newspapers were printed with the miserable story in it.

Happy New Year it wasn't.

Back to jealousy

My overall view of jealousy is that a little bit is not a bad thing. A pang every now and then is, I think, perfectly natural. It might even stop you from ever taking your boyfriend or girlfriend for granted – as long as every time you feel the pang it's immediately followed by that warm feeling of knowing you trust that person implicitly and that they feel the same. Thus you're left feeling lucky to be with this person who is so coveted by others. At that point you can smile too. So jealousy isn't all bad.

A word on male insecurity

A man called Jimmy Soul sang a song called 'If You Wanna Be Happy' in which he gave his fellow men some advice about how to ensure they lived contentedly. His wisdom can be summed up in two of his lines: 'Never make a pretty woman your wife,' and 'Get an ugly girl to marry you.' Jimmy wants men to avoid the stress which, he believes, comes from marrying a beautiful girl, such as the attention she gets from other men.

He might be a man and I'm supposed to be on the side of all men but if this is what he really believes then I think Jimmy Soul is bonkers. Say no to a girl because she's too pretty? I don't know anyone who would do or who has ever done that.

Nice song, though. A very catchy tune.

A final word on jealousy

There will be many times in a relationship where if a guy loves a girl (and I mean really loves her) then every time he looks at her he'll think how amazing she is. And so he will believe that no other guy will be able to look at her and think anything different. There will therefore be times – not all that many, depending on the guy – where he will feel threatened. Take this as a compliment. Don't be angry with him for this because it's proof of how highly he thinks of you. And what's so bad about that? Nothing.

> ## MEN SENSE:
> 1. Jealousy is not always a bad thing.
> 2. If a guy is too jealous and you've tried and failed to reassure him, then as long as you haven't cheated or been disloyal, it's not your fault. It's his problem.
> 3. A racy past is nothing to be ashamed of.
> 4. A nun-like past is nothing to be ashamed of.
> 5. Honesty is always the best policy.

Chapter Twelve

Turning a Fling into a Relationship

- How to maximise your chances of being the one he ends up in a relationship with
- Why you shouldn't push too hard too soon
- How to scare a man away in one easy step
- Don't be afraid to admit you want to be with one guy for the rest of your life
- Why he wants a marriage, not just a wedding

By the time you reach this chapter, you should, I hope, be able to predict the kind of advice I'm going to give. You should be aware that I believe in straightforward tactics like trusting your instincts, using your common sense and not playing it too cool but not rushing in either, things that sound simple but only work when you possess the knowledge to have confidence in yourself and your own mind.

So, where are we now? In terms of what I'm going to tell you, we're nearing the end. Let's imagine you are with a guy you like and you want him to want to turn your fling or first few dates into a relationship. If what you have is good and going well and the timing is right for him, then the chances are this will happen easily and smoothly because it's what he wants too. It may happen more slowly than you want it to (he might be a bit shy, for example) but that's nothing to worry about.

Here are some examples of how to do it but first of all, how not to do it.

Miss Full-On

I know a girl who runs around sleeping with lots of guys. She's usually involved with three or four at any one time (not literally all at the same time, mind you) but not in a I'm-juggling-lots-of-men-aren't-I-cool-and-having-fun-like-a-liberated-woman kind of way. Instead, her scattergun approach is driven by her desire for a boyfriend, and she views all these guys as potential long-term interests.

Her theory is that the more guys she meets, the quicker she'll find the right one. However, this has been going on for years and she's no closer to finding a boyfriend now than she's ever been. She has no problem attracting guys because she's attractive, fun, friendly, bright and has a good heart, but something about her drives them away before these little flings become anything more than that.

There are two reasons why Miss Full-On scares guys away.

Firstly, she is extremely upfront about what she's looking for and tells these guys exactly what her agenda is – namely, finding a boyfriend – on pretty much Date One. This has two consequences. First, the guy feels like he's being auditioned for a role, which is never something we like. And second, he feels like he's being pushed into something, like there is already a plan in place for him. While this might be an extreme example, the solution is applicable to any girl trying to get a guy to commit to her, whether it's two hours after they met, two weeks or two months. And it is this: in the early stages of relationships guys generally like to be happy in the present, the here and now. We don't always think about the future, i.e. where we can see our current relationship going. This doesn't mean we *never* think about the future, far from it, but we do it in our own time, in our own way and at our own speed. However, that doesn't mean you can't affect our decisions. So if you're with a guy who isn't committing to you, then you have to do two things. One is make him happy in the here and now without putting pressure on him, and the other is be independent. Be cool. Pull back in a non-aggressive, non-confrontational way. In both these cases the most important thing to remember is *don't tell him what you're doing*. If he knows what you're up to, he'll realise you're trying to manipulate him and react defensively. But if you do it well, if you make him happy, then while he might not get down on one knee as quickly as you want him to, he will not want to live without you. That's the outcome you want. However, if it doesn't work, back off completely. Tell him you want more than a casual thing and get him out of your life. Be true to yourself.

The second problem with Miss Full-On is that her insecurity makes her too heavy too quickly and these guys get scared off. She tries very hard to project confidence and that effort is obvious. Forced confidence is a sign of insecurity and men do pick up on this.

Miss Full-On – the verdict

It's tempting to say Miss Full-On just needs to meet the right guy and it will all be fine. To an extent that's right. But life isn't that simple or kind. In order to help fate help her, Miss Full-On needs to change the way she thinks and behaves, because the chances of a guy meeting her and thinking she's a diamond in the rough (which she is) and deciding he's the guy who's going to polish her up are minimal. Guys don't work like that. We aren't like girls, who like nothing better than to find a guy who has potential . . . and make him perfect. We don't want to change girls. We like them as they are. We look at girls and think 'she *is* perfect' not 'she *could be* perfect'.

This is why when a guy's girlfriend tells him she's going to do something to her hair his instant reaction is to look panicked and say, 'Don't do that – I like it how it is!' You see, we don't like seeing things we love change. But ninety-nine times out of 100 the same guy will see his girlfriend's new hairdo and love it. In fact he might not even notice. We're a strange bunch.

And there's one other thing Full-On Girl does that she should think about: she goes for players and bad boys. That pattern of behaviour plus her insecurities is unlikely to lead to a happy relationship any time soon.

On the specifics of what Full-On Girl does and what you should avoid, she texts guys regularly (often when they haven't texted her), tries to arrange dates when guys are not trying to see her, texts late at night when she's out and then – and this is a big warning sign – justifies her actions by saying she 'doesn't like playing games'. But letting the guy do the running is not playing games. It's being wise and sensible. That said, following

The Rules most definitely is game playing and you know what I think of that.

The obvious truth about late-night texting

If a single guy who you're not dating regularly (and by not dating I mean either you've been out less than three or four times in quick succession or you've been out a few more times than that over a much longer period) texts you late at night – and we've all done it – then there is one thing I can almost guarantee is not on his mind: he doesn't want you to be his girlfriend. He may want you to come round and get naked with him or he might only be looking for a reaction, something to make him feel a bit less bored and lonely. And if you're up for something similar, i.e. a quick booty call or a bit of cheeky text chat, then by all means play his game. But don't expect this kind of communication to be the prelude to anything other than a casual affair.

Yes, that is a generalisation. But it's also true. Which is why I made the statement so sweeping. And the overall lesson is a simple one: you shouldn't bother analysing too deeply what a guy says in a text message sent late at night. If it's sent at night he's either lonely, bored or horny or a combination of the three. Whatever he is, he's *not* in the market for a relationship with you, so be careful.

Of course, if you're also feeling lonely, bored or horny, go and have fun with him.

The Chat

Late-night texting is, however, completely different if you've had The Chat, that is to say the conversation about the two of you not seeing anyone else.

The Chat – Sally's story

Three weeks after she started seeing Steve, Sally looked through his phone and found out he had slept with someone else a couple of days earlier. She wasn't snooping, by the way, he'd told her to find something for him. Still, the upshot was she saw a text message that showed he'd been in bed with another girl between their last date and the one they were on that day. This did not please Sally. She told Steve how unhappy she was and he said, OK, fine, he could understand she was upset but they hadn't had 'The Chat' about exclusivity yet. Would she like them to stop seeing other people?

'Yes,' Sally said, as she started to calm down. 'I would. And there's something else.'

'Oh yes,' said Steve, 'What's that?'

Sally had slept with someone else as well, only a few days previously. After hearing what he'd been up to, she thought it would be better to tell Steve than keep it to herself. Good on her, I say. But how did Steve react?

He laughed, told her she was crazy for being so upset with him, said he would absolutely not sleep with anyone else again, Sally said the same to him and all was well.

What I find interesting about this story is that Sally and Steve behaved exactly the same way towards each other. As in, they'd both made a conscious decision to sleep with other people because they were still casual and hadn't had The Chat. This situation means one of two things (and I can't tell you which because Sally and Steve have only been together for a couple of months as I write this, so I don't know how the story ends). Either:

1. Sally and Steve don't actually like each other that much and their fling will fizzle out in the not too distant future, or
2. Their coupling will be very successful because they have similar ways of handling the beginning of a relationship.

Had one of them been like me – I won't lay a finger on another girl after I've met someone I really like, even if The Chat hasn't happened – then things may have been tricky. But because they had both behaved the same then the playing field was level.

This is close to being two wrongs making a right territory by the way, which is never healthy. But only close. Had they both slept with other people two years into their relationship then I expect they'd have broken up but at this stage, when they'd only just met, they could both rationalise it and understand because they saw their own behaviour reflected in the other person. All power to them and I'll be fascinated to see how it pans out.

Men secrets

If you've just slept with a new guy (or are about to) and are worried about the exclusivity thing, there's absolutely nothing wrong with saying to him something like: 'I'm not putting pressure on you but I wanted you to know that whatever this turns out to be, I'm not sleeping with anyone else and so I hope you won't either.' If the guy likes you, he'll think, 'Brilliant – she only wants me!' and be very happy. And I mean genuinely delighted. If he kicks up a fuss about not wanting to be tied down (metaphorically), then at least you know where you stand.

And one other thing, when you say these words, don't use the word 'boyfriend'. Not even in a way intended to be completely non-aggressive, as in 'I'm not saying you're my boyfriend but . . .' Most guys won't bat an eyelid but some would, so don't use that word. It's just not worth the risk.

The No-Chat Chat

I know a couple who met, started seeing each other and nine months later were living together without so much as a single word uttered by either of them about whether they were dating, seeing each other, going out, stepping out, courting or even betrothed. Nothing. Not a word.

Why?

Because the No-Chat Girl was clever.

The No-Chat Girl realised that the No-Chat Guy couldn't be pushed into anything. She knew he was headstrong and did not like being told what to do. So the No-Chat Girl didn't tell him what to do. Over those nine months they saw each other regularly, gradually more and more, and the No-Chat Girl played her hand perfectly. She spent a lot of time with the No-Chat Guy and behaved exactly like a girlfriend would, just without ever putting a label on what they were to each other. She was relaxed. No pressure on him, nothing. And neither got even remotely involved with anyone else along the way, unlike Sally and Steve.

The overview

Thus if two people really like each other then their goals will be the same – i.e. to be in an exclusive relationship – and that means if they're honest and open about their feelings for each other then my theory is that in general their lives together will fall into place.

Isn't it amazing how complicated things can be so simple?

The big commitment

You should never be afraid to admit that your ultimate goal is that one day you want to be with one person for the rest of your life. Not only is this an important part of being true to yourself but most guys feel exactly the same. So if you find yourself dating one who doesn't or even who says he doesn't (this may be because his timing is off or you're simply not the right one), then he's not worth your time, let alone your love.

Trust in men. No, really, you can

We men don't discuss this much between us, but we all know that trust is just about the most important thing in a relationship. Trust is what makes two people truly special to each other, what puts their relationship above those they have with anyone else, friend or family. Trust is what enables a couple to create a private world to which no one else is allowed access, where things the two of them feel, say and do are kept secret, reserved only for the eyes and ears of the person they're in love with. This, in my view, is a fundamental part of how a happy couple should look after and respect each other. It's also not simply about being faithful – although that's a given – it's about being *the* special person to each other so that you both have that special bond.

You know this already, don't you?

So, you might ask, why am I telling you this?

There's one reason and one reason alone: because you might never have heard a guy say it before, even though we all think it.

Why do men cheat?

I knew I was going to have to answer this one at some point. So here goes.

There are many reasons why some men can't keep it in their trousers but because I like giving simple answers to complicated questions, I'm not going to get bogged down by trying to explain every single one of them.

The basic rule is this: in general if a relationship is healthy, i.e.

if two people look after each other and understand each other's needs, be they sexual or otherwise, then a man won't cheat. If something goes wrong, if the relationship breaks down, then that's when it's possible that the man (or the woman – they cheat too, remember) will be unfaithful. Of course relationships go through ups and downs and most men understand this and will behave accordingly – that is to say properly and in a non-cheating way. But some won't.

Even this rule isn't reliable because some men cheat when they're in happy relationships.

So what kind of man cheats?

All kinds. That is to say, there isn't a certain type who will or won't so it is very difficult to give a precise answer to that question. A guy who slept with lots of girls in his younger days and therefore seems like an obvious candidate might meet a special girl and never look at another one again. Equally, a guy who was a nerdy virgin until his mid-twenties, married young and who subsequently became rich and successful could suddenly find it much easier to get women and decide to make up for lost time in spite of his marital status. He also might stay faithful forever. There is no pattern.

What it boils down to is this: some men just cheat. Some men are capable of making that 'I'm going to sleep with someone else' decision while others won't. The best advice I can give you is to keep your relationship healthy in every way you can and trust your instincts. Assume your guy isn't going to cheat until and unless you have reason to think otherwise.

Are men motivated solely by sex? No. But if they're not getting enough, then it can warp our minds and make us do strange things, like cheat on girls we love, because, as I've explained before, sex is not just about sex to guys. It's just the icing on the happy cake, if that makes sense.

I read an article in the *Daily Mail* recently by a playwright, Peadar De Burca, who interviewed 250 men who'd cheated on their wives. His conclusions were fascinating. I'll pick on one in particular: 'I imagined they'd be living exciting, glamorous lives. But nothing could be further from the truth. If one thing's certain, affairs don't make you happy. Once I'd dug beneath the boasting and bravado, I was stunned by just how insecure most of these love cheats were. Most admitted they weren't even driven by sex. They just wanted something to fill their empty lives.'

I agree completely. It's unhappy people who cheat and cheating only makes them more unhappy.

The responses below the online version of the story were also fascinating. The usual 'men are idiots' and 'women cheat just as much as men' (both of which are probably true) were followed by this from a woman who wanted to simplify things:

'Men cheat because their wives stop having interesting sex with them. End of story. The women think that they can give up sex because they have been married xx years but the men still have the desire. So the men last as long as they can and eventually they give up and find another woman. It really is *that* simple. This story misses that entirely and concentrates on the poor old wife who, after getting her man and her house and her lifestyle ... gave up keeping her man interested. And yes, it is up to us women, not the men. Men are stupid compared to us and are controlled by the brain between their legs, so it is up to us to control them.'

This is a simplistic view but not an entirely inaccurate one. If a man is in a happy relationship (and a happy relationship is one which, among other things, is sexually satisfying) then the vast majority of men won't cheat. If he's not happy, the chances of him being unfaithful go up. But it's not as simple as the old saying that a man is only as faithful as his opportunities. That isn't true. We're far more complicated than that.

So how do you stop a man from cheating? Make sure your relationship is a happy one. That's all you can do. And all a man can do to stop his girlfriend or wife from cheating is by doing everything he can to make their relationship a happy one. I told you I liked simple answers to complicated questions.

And if you're cheated on, how do you get over that? Well, the only useful thing I can say on that subject is that you shouldn't take it personally. Guys who cheat will do it no matter who they are with at that time of their lives. A guy who cheats in his early twenties might not ever do it again because he grows up. But other guys won't ever grow up and if you happen to be with one of these guys then as long as you're doing everything you can to keep your relationship happy, then it's nothing to do with you and is most definitely not your fault.

For any girls who've been recently cheated on that might not be much use but I'm afraid it's all I have.

Too much jealousy is a killer

Someone once told me that people who are excessively jealous regarding their boyfriend or girlfriend usually have something to hide, namely their own romantic indiscretions.

Do I believe this? No, I don't.

The most jealous girl I've ever known used to check my phone every day, look over my work notes to see who I'd been talking to, demand to know exactly where I was at every moment of every day and would accuse me of fancying just about every female I came into contact with. Including her mother. Seriously, she accused me of fancying her mother.

I do not believe she was driven to this insane level of jealousy by the fact she was hiding some other boyfriend away. Some people are simply like that – they cannot stop their insecurities boiling over and do not have the emotional intelligence to understand that if you behave towards your boyfriend as she did – basically trying to control everything I did, down to who my friends were – you'll end up making him miserable and then, almost inevitably, losing him. And I'm sure this works the other way round as well.

Trust story – Rita, Roger and Miss X

Rita's boyfriend Roger has a close female friend, Miss X, who makes Rita very angry (please note that was angry not jealous). Rita trusts Roger totally but thinks Miss X is after him. Miss X tries to hang out with Roger when Rita is not around and is all over him when Rita is. Roger does not encourage Miss X, he does not communicate with her behind Rita's back, he does not pretend he's seeing someone else when he sees Miss X (which is almost always for quick lunches during the workday) and finds it hard to see what the problem is. To him, Rita is the girl he loves while Miss X is simply his friend. But Rita feels like Miss X is constantly trying to shoulder her out of the way so she can take her place with Roger.

What should Rita do?

Actually, it's quite simple. Rita genuinely trusts Roger and rightly so. This means she shouldn't make a huge fuss because he has done nothing wrong (Miss X was his friend before he met Rita) and to Roger they are only ever going to be friends. Even if Rita didn't exist he wouldn't want to hook up with Miss X.

If there was any history between them she might have something to worry about (more if it was casual than a long-term thing, actually – sex is the theme there), but with no history, she doesn't need to worry, especially because she trusts her boyfriend so much. Rita has never questioned how he feels or how honest he is being with her.

That said, if she senses something mutual, then she should worry. That's a time to listen to your instincts. I know a girl whose boyfriend had a close friend he'd known since they were children. The girlfriend rarely saw the female friend, even though she and the boyfriend were close and she was with him for two years. Whenever she mentioned this friend, her boyfriend always insisted there was nothing between them, that they had only ever been and only ever would be friends.

But after two years he dumped her and very soon after got together with this old friend. The now-ex believes that the girl got to a stage of her life where she was ready for this guy to become her boyfriend and that on some level they'd both known that moment would come. When it did, my friend was history, immediately. I feel so sorry for this girl. She was basically conned throughout those two years. Again, her instincts told her something wasn't right and her instincts were absolutely correct.

One final word on Rita and Roger: sooner or later one of two things will happen. Either Roger will be less interested in hanging out with Miss X as things get more serious with Rita or, unbelievable as this might seem to Rita, Miss X will get a boyfriend. Either one of those events will mean Miss X sees Roger less often. And that should make Rita happy. So Rita should keep calm and carry on trusting Roger. Don't make a huge song and dance about Miss X. Rita should rise above her. Roger will love her for that. Rita doesn't need to compete because Roger already loves her.

Guys not trusting other guys

My friend told me this story: *'My ex had a very close male friend who she'd known for years. I liked him because he was fun but I didn't trust him. The thing was, he and my girlfriend had pulled many, many times over the years. I knew exactly what had gone on because she told me – she always really liked him and wanted him to be her boyfriend but all he did was grab her when he was drunk and felt a bit frisky.*

'I don't know if he led her on or said anything to her about them getting together properly but even so, when it's so obvious that a girl likes you, it's not right to take advantage of her for five years, especially when she's supposed to be one of your closest friends. To be honest, we've all gone with girls we weren't that keen on simply because they were up for it but I don't know many guys who would string someone along for five years, especially someone who's supposed to be a friend. That was out of order.

'Even after all that, when we got together she was always very protective of him and got very, very defensive if I was anything other than complimentary about him. The worst thing, actually, was that whenever he was around, she treated me like I was invisible. I didn't try to stop her from seeing him because I didn't want to be that jealous guy but looking back I kind of wish I had,

because I hated the situation. I should have spoken up because it ate away at me over the time we were together.

'Believe it or not, I actually tried to like him at first. But that soon wore off. Once, during a stupid drinking game, he asked me what the best sex I'd ever had was while my ex was sitting right next to me because she was playing the same game. He looked at me and smiled knowingly and at that moment I felt like throwing a chair at his head.

'You see, guys know full well how badly other guys are capable of behaving. We're all the same in some ways, it's just some of us have different boundaries and stop ourselves from doing things because we realise girls can get hurt by our behaviour. As far as I was concerned this guy was a loser from that moment on. He'd sat there and deliberately reminded me that he'd slept with my girlfriend and the implication was that he thought she still wanted him.

'I broke up with my ex years ago now and it wasn't because of him, although I don't think her attitude to him helped the general state of our relationship. I don't think she cheated on me with him (in fact I'm as close to certain as it's possible to be that she didn't) but I always thought he was the kind of guy who would have slept with her while we were together if he could, if only to prove to himself that he could still have her when he wanted.

'She was a great girl and I really, really hope she's clear of him now because that guy was bad news. It is one of my great regrets that I never got to punch him in the face. I'd have enjoyed that.'

This friend of mine ended up happy, by the way. But with another girl.

Men and other men (no, not in that way)

If a guy who has boundaries (see reference above) knows another guy who does not have boundaries, he won't trust him. Another friend of mine knows a guy who he literally will not leave his girlfriend alone with. Not because he doesn't trust his girlfriend but because this guy, who my friend gets on with, cannot be trusted even with his mates' girlfriends. His friends have all known this for years.

What kind of idiot is he? And why do his friends carry on hanging out with him? I'm not sure I understand. All I can say is guys who have known each other for a long time are very loyal to each other.

Why guys worry about other guys

When a guy really likes a girl, and I mean really likes her, every time he looks at her he will think how amazing she is and that he can't believe his luck (look, for example, at how David Cameron looks at his wife Samantha – there is a man who is constantly thinking how lucky he is). An extension of this for many men at one time or another is to think that if this is how he feels then surely every other guy will feel the same. And if every other guy feels the same about his girl, sooner or later one will try to take her from him. And the more who try, the more likely it is that one will succeed. So runs the thought process of the loved-up but insecure male.

Do loved-up girls feel the same about their guys? I expect so.

MEN SENSE:

1. Not all guys are bad.
2. Some guys wholeheartedly disapprove of other guys' behaviour.
3. Male friendship is a strange thing. You won't always understand it.
4. Some men just cheat. It's not your fault.
5. Always assume the best about people, while being careful.

Conclusion

When I sat down to write my final column I felt unusually emotional. I realised how much I would miss everything associated with it: the writing, the fun I had because of it (which was often my friends laughing at me), the fact that lots of people read it and, I don't mind admitting, the ego boost of seeing my face on a newspaper page every week (even though the photo they used was terrible). And so, as the tears dripped on to my keyboard (not quite true but you get the picture), I decided to share the wisdom I'd gained over the past two years. I was in my twenty-sixth month of being single and this is what I wrote:

'It doesn't matter how you meet someone you like. You just have to give yourself the best possible chance of it happening and the best way to do that is to stop worrying about rejection, which is the biggest lesson I've learned from this. Just about everyone – male and female – is far too scared of being rejected. Guys, remember there are no rules about where, when or how to ask a girl out. If you want to do it, just do it. And if she says no, that doesn't matter. Far better to try and fail than to not try at all. And anyway, it's a lot of fun. Girls need to understand that sometimes there is literally nothing they can do to change a guy's mind. Lame as it sounds, timing is almost always to blame for him going cold and that is nothing to do with you. Don't beat yourself up. It's not worth it. Just carry on having fun and being nice to people and you'll win in the end. And to everyone: be honest and don't lie or cheat. It's not worth it.'

The end of the beginning

Over those twenty-six months, the pressure of writing my column every week meant I thought about being single a *lot*. I thought about how to meet girls, why I should meet girls, why I shouldn't meet girls, how to meet the wrong girls, how to meet the right girl, where I should try to meet her, why I wasn't meeting her and then, finally, why I should stop trying to meet her.

That last one came shortly after the time my column ended. I was single at that point (apologies to anyone who read it and thought differently – I may have misled you for the sake of a nice ending to nearly two years of dating stories) and around then I had a low moment when I realised that if I hadn't met the right girl after everything that had happened, all the thinking, talking, writing, dating, being set up and so on, how was it ever going to happen? What else could I do? Where would I find her? I had no idea.

That's not me being self-pitying or over-dramatic. I honestly did not have a clue about where or how I was going to meet the girl I wanted to spend the rest of my life with. I could not see where she would possibly appear from. As a result I deliberately gave up trying. I thought to myself, oh well, nothing you've done so far has worked so you might as well stop all the fuss, relax and put your heart in the lap of the gods. Accept that it's out of your hands. I shrugged my shoulders and decided to simply get on with my life and enjoy myself. Luckily for me that wasn't too hard because work was going much better, I had plenty of friends, it was summer and I had lots of fun plans. Life was generally very good.

And that was when something unexpected happened.

At the end of August, nearly two months after the column ended, I went to a wedding. Lots of my friends were going, people I hadn't seen for ages and who I hadn't been with as a group for several years, so it promised to be a great weekend. I was very happy and the fact I was now one of very few single people in the party didn't bother me at all.

On the Friday night of the wedding weekend, with a big smile on my face and feeling really excited about the next few days, I walked into the pub where everyone was meeting for the night-before booze-up, saw a girl I hadn't met before in the group, felt a connection with her immediately, before we'd even talked, and to cut a fairly short story even shorter, that was it.

If you ask Charlotte, however (and she has her say at the end of the book), she'll say I didn't actually speak to her until late on the Saturday evening and it was only an accidental collision between us on the dance floor that broke the ice. This is true up to a point. For a start that collision wasn't accidental – I'm not that bad a dancer – and while no one introduced us I knew we were going to meet properly at some point that day. I was simply biding my time and waiting for the right moment.

Anyway, after that we became very close very quickly and I

found something I'd come to believe I would never have at a time when I wasn't even looking for it any more.

That experience affected the writing of this entire book in a way which I hope is obvious, because once I met Charlotte, I understood much more clearly what had been going on in my head and my life for the previous two-and-a-half years, how I'd changed and grown and learned things about myself and the world. The journey from breaking up with Girlfriend Y to meeting Charlotte suddenly made sense. I understood what happened and, more importantly, how it happened. And I became an optimist. I now believe in happy endings.

The main lesson is this: if you've been single for a while (longer than you wanted to be, at least) then the best way to put an end to that is to stop worrying about it and focus on other things, namely enjoying your life. Then, once you're happy and having a good time as a single person, that's when unexpected things can happen. Great things with hearts and bells on.

Without me realising it, that's exactly what happened in my life. When I met Charlotte, the time was right for me (I'd been single for long enough) and I wasn't doing the column any more. This took some pressure off me because I didn't have to think about being single and why I was single *every week of my life* (the column was fun but it got a bit draining after a while, believe me).

So in the background the pieces were falling into place for me to be ready to meet someone – general contentment in life, no pressure, etc. But there is one other factor that no matter of preparation or emotional wisdom can affect or force. And that is luck. Pure, simple good fortune. The fact is I was very, very lucky that Charlotte came along at all, let alone when she did. I did not make her appear at that moment. She just did, for reasons I can't predict, control or even understand.

Of course, what that means is I can't claim to have discovered the true secret to successful dating because I cannot guarantee that anyone else will end up where I am now if they decide to follow my advice and do as I did. Nothing I say can be sure to make the right person appear for anyone else because none of us can control luck and we all need it to end up happy. All I could do was put myself in a place where if the right person came along, I was ready for her.

And that, I believe, is all I or any other single person can do – put ourselves in the right place and hope the right person comes along at the right time, following the principle that luck is simply the perfect meeting of preparation and opportunity. Hopefully this book will help you get to that right place emotionally (where you realise you're confident, wise and happy in your life and yourself) and physically (out having fun and meeting people rather than sitting at home moping around) so that when your opportunity comes along you are ready, just like I was.

B

Of course you want to know what happened to B. Well, over the course of my time as a single man, he pulled lots and lots of girls, as usual. And in the first few months of the time I've been with Charlotte (at the time of writing it's been just over a year), he carried on in the same vein.

But then he stopped. There was no particular reason, no one girl who made him change. He just didn't want to do that any more. No, he hasn't met anyone yet but he is getting closer all the time to being ready. I asked if he would mind explaining what was happening to him but he said he couldn't because he didn't know himself. In that way he's like I was when I finished writing my column but before I met Charlotte – going through a process that you can only really understand when you reach the end.

It will happen for B eventually, I'm sure of it.

A few thoughts for single girls who are bored of being single

If you've been single for a while and are not finding the right guy, then the chances are you're actually not ready to find him. And if you look at your life and think the one thing you need to make it perfect is a guy, then you're definitely not ready. You need to be happy with yourself before you can find the right relationship.

The fact is you have to learn to love yourself before someone can love you. I know that sounds cheesy but it's true, as much for guys as for girls. No book can do this for you but I can help point you in the right direction. I believe loving yourself comes from accepting yourself. You are what you are and the sooner you deal with that the better. There are no alternatives or second chances.

Of course, if you don't like something about yourself which is changeable, change it. That might be your job, your hair colour or even your weight. But if you don't like something you *can't* change, then stop worrying about it because you can't do anything about it and the longer you let it make you unhappy, the longer you'll be unhappy. So accept it and accept yourself. Take control.

Another potential consequence of not accepting yourself is that if someone good loves you and you don't love yourself, it's possible that your lack of confidence will lead to you not trusting him or believing him when he says how he feels and that is a very dangerous state of affairs. So respect and love yourself because it is hard for anyone to love you in the way you want to be loved if you don't already love yourself.

And remember, confidence is attractive and self-fulfilling. Appear confident and you will be confident. If it's absolutely necessary then fake it till you make it.

If you keep meeting the wrong guys – whether they're the same type of wrong guys or simply ones who are unsuitable for different reasons – then it's you who needs to change. Take a look at yourself first and ask some questions, like do you know what you want from a guy? Where do you meet these wrong guys? If, say, you meet them in clubs, what do you wear in these clubs? And which clubs do you go to? Are you drunk when you go to these clubs? If so, consider this: if you had to make an important decision in your life – be it buying a new car or house, whether to leave your job or even emigrate – would you make that decision after downing a bottle of wine and a couple of double vodka and Red Bulls? Of course you wouldn't. So why do you think you can make any sort of decent decision in the same state when you go looking for a man in a nightclub?

Exactly, it doesn't make sense.

Most people who have made mistakes with the wrong person – and pretty well everyone has – have usually been too drunk to realise it was a mistake and thus woke up regretting it.

It's no wonder girls who behave like that can't find anyone! So, bearing in mind that looking for guys in clubs probably isn't the best way to start but that going out and having fun is always a good idea, when you do go out, stop looking for guys. Focus on making sure you feel good about yourself and enjoy your evening without being on the hunt. And FYI, drunk girls are not very attractive to guys anyway.

The more questions like these you ask, the more you will learn about yourself and the more opportunities you'll have to make changes that will benefit you. But remember this, too: time spent with the wrong guys is not time wasted as long as you learn from it. If you don't learn from these experiences, you'll repeat them and never be happy.

I've heard several single girls say that they might not know what they want in a guy but they do know what they don't want. If you're one of these girls (and even if you're not this can be useful), write a list of those things you don't want on one side of paper and then on the other side write a list of what you do want. If you can't think of anything just write the opposites of what you do want. For example, you might not want a boyfriend who gets drunk five times a week so put on the other side that you want someone who drinks in moderation. Or if you don't want someone who's thoughtless, put on the other side that you want a guy who is considerate and kind. See what I'm getting at?

When you think about the kind of guy you want, focus on the positives, not negatives. That attitude will help you move forwards. Once you've worked out what it is you want, write it all down and lock the bit of paper away somewhere. That way your thoughts have been released and your mind will be clear. You will now be ready when the right one appears.

Don't change for a guy and don't expect him to change either. I don't mean things like hair, clothes or tidiness (most guys benefit from some female attention in those areas, at least I did). I mean behaviour, friends and other fundamentals of your personality. If you find yourself wanting to change fundamental things in a guy or find a guy trying to change fundamental things in you, get rid of the guy.

Don't let a guy be horrible to you. If one does treat you badly, ask yourself how you'd feel if a guy did that to your daughter or your sister or best friend. Imagine you're your own mother and know how mean a guy is being to you. How would you feel?

If you make rules for yourself, make them positive. For example, instead of 'don't sleep with him on the first date', make the rule 'sleep with him after at least four dates and if the time is right'. No use of 'don't', 'can't' or 'won't' is allowed in this context. Be positive, always.

Finally, here's a story. A friend of mine was single and dateless for about two years. He made no effort to meet girls at all. The reason was simply that he wasn't happy in his life and so wasn't ready for a relationship. After two years, something in him changed and he became content. He decided he'd like to meet a girl so he joined an online dating site and over a weekend had four dates (Friday night, Saturday lunch, Saturday night and Sunday lunch, if you want the details). He wasn't interested in any of them. On the Monday morning a new girl started in his office, and guess what? Eighteen months on they've just bought a house together.

All this goes to show is that if you want a relationship, you have to put yourself in the right places to make it happen, mentally, physically and even technologically: mentally by learning to love yourself, physically by not locking yourself away from the world and technologically because online dating is the easiest way to get dates ever invented.

So give fate a helping hand and wonderful things can happen.

Conclusion – the secrets summed up

By now you've heard all the dating stories I collected and you've heard my thoughts on them all. I hope you've been reassured by stories of people who made mistakes far worse than any of the minor indiscretions you managed and that you know there are some good guys out there, despite some of us being pigs.

And I hope you still think being single can be a lot of fun. Being single doesn't mean you lose your ability to make people laugh and your friends will still love you if you don't have a man in your life. Single life should be brilliant. It's your chance to meet and date as many men as you want, to have fun, to make mistakes, laugh about them and learn from them until eventually you work out what and who it is you want.

So to finish with, here are what I believe to be the most important points from the entire book:

1. Be selfish – don't put other people's happiness ahead of your own, unless they're your children.
2. Don't make excuses for guys who treat you badly.
3. Don't let a relationship get off on the wrong foot – be who you are from the start.
4. There is no one-size-fits-all set of rules for guys and girls and dating. Everyone is different. Work out your own rules.

5. Part of the fun of being single and dating is making mistakes. Make sure you learn from yours and never be ashamed of them. And keep at it – Rome wasn't built in a day.

6. Trust your common sense, yourself and your instincts. They and you are much more powerful than you think.

Thanks for reading and good luck.

Appendix A

A Few Words from Charlotte

A couple of years ago my old flatmate from university, Pip, had an engagement party to which I was invited even though she knew I would know *no one* there. Her fiancé Olly should have had a lot of friends coming, a couple of whom were single. But as my luck would have it, they didn't turn up. Of course, this didn't stop the happy, gooey couple from trying to pass on their happiness to their lonely single friend. Ooh, who could they set me up with, they pondered. 'A nice, single girl who always goes for the bad boys, let's set her up with one of Olly's friends! Who is there? John? Hmm, maybe not, he doesn't live in London . . . Mark? Perhaps too short for her . . . Ooh, I know, how about Humfrey?'

Humfrey?

Really?

Do people even have names like that anymore? I mean, I know I come from a comical background of funny names – my parents are called Peter and Piper and our surname is Cockey – but Humfrey? How odd. They told me to take a look at the next Tuesday's issue of *London Lite* to see his picture on the column he wrote. I was to let them know if they should set us up.

Two days later, I completely forgot to get the paper but was so excited after they bigged him up to me that I told my flatmate that she had to go and get a copy of it on her way home from work (I was already home and it was raining, and I wasn't *that* desperate.) So Sunita came in with a damp copy of *London Lite* and we scrambled through it to find Humfrey Hunter's column – and there he was. Sunita said, 'Oooh he's nice looking.' I, on the other hand, decided to just close the paper and continue watching TV because my expectations had gotten the better of me and I was disappointed. (It was a terrible photo – even at the shoot for that picture, Humfrey told them to use any picture, except *that* one. The bastards.) Sunita thought I should meet him anyway, but I didn't want to be any more disappointed so I decided not to. Besides, he was writing a *dating* column so who was he, the female Carrie Bradshaw? I'd seen enough *Sex and the City* episodes to know that I didn't want any intimate details about our date to be narrated to the whole of London. How embarrassing would that be? And how many other girls was he dating? Clearly he wasn't looking for a proper girlfriend. I mean, what's the point of a dating column if you're in a relationship? So I came to my own conclusions and decided that I was better off going out with my friends than going on a date with him.

Flash forward through fifteen months of more dismal dates and Olly and Pip got married. I had always pondered about Humfrey Hunter and whether I should have gone on a date with him. Now I was finally going to meet him. I got the train up alone the night before and Pip arranged for the photographer to take me over to the pub where they were having pre-wedding drinks and food, when finally Humfrey Hunter walked in. Pip pointed him out immediately, 'That's Humfrey who we wanted to set you up with,' she said.

Oh, I thought. And then, Oops.

As the old milk advert used to say, watch out, watch out, there's a Humfrey about . . . and finally this one was about. I managed to get on his table for dinner that night, although he never spoke to me (and there was only one person sat in between us). However, I could tell there was something there.

The next morning, although she wasn't coming to the wedding, Sunita came to meet me as we were in her home town, and I told her all about Humfrey Hunter and how I felt something there, and that he looked nothing like his stupid column photo. He was tall, had a lovely smile, beautiful eyes and an incredibly deep voice. I hadn't even spoken to him and I was already thinking about him in such a stalker-ish way. I could tell Sunita was a bit wary: she'd had more than two years of my dissecting of guys and 'relationships', of which none came to anything, mainly because I always tended to go for the guys who I knew I couldn't get. But two weeks before the wedding I'd made a change. I'd decided to stop all the messing around, stop hurting myself and had got rid of those guys who used me to make themselves feel better and took advantage of a girl who didn't know what she wanted. I'd had enough. I didn't deserve to be treated this way, I knew that one day I would meet someone who would love me for who I was and not try and change me. I was done with all of that, so I had to get those kinds of men out of my life. And so I did.

And it's true, once you clear out all your demons, find out what you want and start respecting yourself, then the universe has a funny way of rewarding you. You may have to wait, or it may happen like it did to me in just two weeks, all I know is it only really happens when you are ready.

So, the whole time at the wedding, the church, the drinks,

the dinner, and most of the dancing, Mr Humfrey Hunter didn't talk to me (even though he knew I was completely alone and knew no one). He smiled at me once but that was it. I must have read the signs wrong the night before, he clearly wasn't interested. But then why was he always on the dance floor when I was? Why did he keep looking at me? Why didn't he just *talk* to me?

In the end he got me the easy way: the guy I was dancing with span me round too many times and I ended up in Humfrey Hunter's arms and that was it. The sparks, the sickly butterfly feeling in my gut, the weak knees, and the cheesy lines, which at the time I thought were *so* romantic. And when we kissed outside, the groom came along and peed right next to us and said, in a drunken slur, 'I predicted six weeks ago that this would happen!'

And that was it. Humfrey is now my boyfriend and my best friend. We respect each other, we love each other, we don't try to change each other and above all we have fun. Just two months after setting eyes on each other we went on holiday to Antigua for two weeks, which we were both terrified about. When we booked it we weren't even 'official'. I was worried about scaring him off when I suggested the holiday but he was up for it and it was definitely a test for me. Unless I'm with my family, going on holiday with friends had usually ended up in some sort of disaster. But with Humfrey it was perfect, even with the food poisoning I got pretty early in the holiday. And he's still here.

I sometimes wonder if we would have got together had we met straight after the engagement party. I don't think we would. Neither of us was ready for a serious relationship then, we both had baggage and more lessons we needed to learn from other people. It just goes to show that once two people have dealt with that baggage and been taught their lessons, fate, or whatever you want to call it, has a way of guiding them to each other. I also wonder what would have happened if I had chickened out of going to the three-day wedding alone. Would Humfrey Hunter and I have ever met? Maybe not, which is why one of the important things to learn when you're single is to be brave and go for it. I read somewhere recently that 90% of what happens to us in our lifetime is from the decisions we make in life. So maybe we all make our own fate. You have to look at yourself and find out what you are really looking for to be happy. But, as I learned, you also have to be willing to let go of all the past and live in the present, enjoying every moment, not wasting time on the guys who just use you or you know deep down are wrong for you. And above all respect yourself.

Humfrey has two sisters who he loves very dearly, so I know how much he respects women, and everything he has said in this book is true – the male perspective is not as complicated as us girls think it is. It is quite harsh to read some of the stories and situations as I know we have all been there at some point, but I think it is good to know how these things can play out through other people's experiences before it is too late, so we can think about how we handle them ourselves in future.

To be honest, it's a shame for me that this book is coming out now. I used to hate dating, the whole idea of it made me feel sick. I wasn't very good at it – I always went out with guys who I had met once before in a dark club only to find them repulsive in daylight. I never really had the confidence to go on dates with guys I liked, I was too worried about if they liked me or not and I hated having to wait for them to text me to ask me out. You learn so much from meeting different guys and with a book like this I'd have known much more much earlier, which would have been very useful.

I've always believed that the more you date other guys, the more you will realise what you actually want. And being single for a while is so important. We all need to get to know ourselves so we can understand what makes us happy. I know a couple of girls who on reaching the 'grand old age' of twenty-five broke up with their boyfriends and then panicked at the thought that they were going to be single for the rest of their lives, so very quickly went out with the next guy who came along without even a moment's reflection on what had happened in the previous relationship. Of course they ended up being miserable and wondering why they kept meeting the wrong person. For what it's worth, my advice is not to rush things, and to take some time to understand what you really want – even if it takes a while for him to come along.

I think sometimes some of us girls can be quite shallow and have some kind of unobtainable ideal of who we want to date in our head, but sometimes we need to get to know the guy before making any judgements about him. When the right one does come along, it won't matter if he doesn't buy you flowers (it was one year before Humfrey bought me any flowers and they were £3.99 from Sainsburys – I rest my case) or wears green chinos or socks with sandals. What matters above all else, is how he makes you feel about yourself.

And above all, if your friends want to set you up with one of their nice friends, no matter what his name happens to be, don't research him beforehand and don't judge him on one dodgy photo. Just go for it.

Appendix B

Men in Relationships

While researching this book, I asked countless girls the question: 'What is the trouble with men?' I wanted to know what it was about men that most bothered, irritated, annoyed or confused girls. Most of the issues raised by the answers have been covered already. But there is one category left out of this book: men in relationships. Therefore below are the top twenty-five answers to the question: 'What is the trouble with men in relationships?', and my responses to them.

Some of the points made in the replies apply to all men, including me. But others clearly say less about men and more about one particular man, namely the husband or boyfriend of whoever it was who sent in the response.

So here to complete your education are the twenty-five most common troubles with men in relationships . . .

1. They believe house fairies (i.e. women) wash all the dishes and clothes, empty the bins and fill the fridge.

Whoever wrote this needs to re-evaluate how her household is run. What she doesn't seem to realise is men don't mind doing their fair share. What they do mind, though, is being told they aren't doing something the right way. Whether it's rinsing the washing-up in the wrong temperature water, folding clothes badly or buying the wrong make of pasta, being told we're doing something badly makes us not want to do it at all. Or anything else. On the one side you have the many girls who have trouble accepting that their way of doing something is not the only right way (there are lots of you, be honest) and on the other side there are men who don't like being treated as inferior beings when it comes to running a house (all of us – we're not children any more). And anyway, it's the twenty-first century which means we'll happily do our bit and more. This girl should strike a deal with her man: she won't treat him like an incompetent employee and he'll do more around the house.

2. They expect praise for completing a tiny task despite taking ages to get it done.

Yes indeed we do. That's because there are three things we love getting from our girlfriends more than anything else and they are food, praise and sex. If you make sure your man has enough of those three things then whichever man is lucky enough to share your life will be a happy one.

3. They are incapable of noticing their own bodily odours, foul bins or blocked sinks — but have sharper noses than any sniffer dog when there's a roast in the oven.

There are some smells that don't provoke extreme reactions in men. We will put the rubbish out if it stinks. We will unblock a sink if you ask us to. But unless the stench is literally melting our sinuses, we'll ignore it. You must accept that the threshold of what's acceptable is different in the male nose. That's all – simple biology.

Equally, if we smell something we like, such as a roast, we will get very, very excited, which is why the old and true saying about the way to a man's heart being through his stomach has been said so often by so many people over so many years. And if you're cooking up something special and we seem happy about it, you should be happy too because if you're the one who made that wonderful-smelling food, well, if you're not in our hearts already you won't be far away.

4. They jump in with fix-it solutions when we just want to be heard – they don't seem to understand we like whingeing.

I've heard this complaint before from both guys and girls so I know it's not only men who are guilty. In fact it's happened to me while speaking to girls and I know how frustrating it is when you're the one doing the talking and the only thing you want is to be listened to. All you can do is tell whoever it is you're talking to that the one thing you want to do is let off steam and get something off your chest. Tell them you don't need a solution, that all you need is to say what you want to say, be listened to and move on and hope they remember for next time.

If you need a positive side until that lesson kicks in, remember that if they're offering solutions, at least they're trying to help, which means they care.

5. They are incapable of thinking beyond the next week and arranging holidays or fun things for us to do.

Rubbish. Men do think in a more short-term way about what they're doing but we do like to make plans and have things to look forward to. Whoever said this needs to plan those things in a different way with the man she's complaining about. Don't put him on the spot by telling him to go and plan something fun for you to do together. Men don't like being put on the spot. We don't do well when pressurised by a girl in that way. Work out plans together. Buy a listings magazine or look online together. Whatever you do, whether it's the arranging or the enjoying, do it together.

And stop complaining because the attitude behind the complaint is all wrong. If all you have to moan about is that your boyfriend leaves arranging holidays to you, which means *you* get to decide where you go on holiday, then you really need to stop being so negative and focus on the positives in your relationship. Does he cheat? No. Is he kind and honest? Yes. Is he a bit laid-back about making holiday plans? Yes. Does that mean you get to go exactly where you want when the pair of you head off abroad? Yes. Seriously, stop moaning. Right now. You're a lucky girl.

6. They don't remember or care about things we've planned or birthdays and anniversaries.

On my birthdays, before my friends started settling down and getting married, I could always tell which of them had girlfriends and which were single. How? Easy – the ones with girlfriends gave me birthday cards and sometimes even presents while the single ones always came empty-handed. And did I mind? No, of course not. The fact is guys don't buy each other birthday cards. Nor do we expect them. But when a guy has a girlfriend, birthday cards appear and that's nice too. We appreciate them. But if our friends don't get us one, we don't mind. Of course we enjoy going out on our birthdays and expect our friends to show up but apart from being bought a drink or two, we don't expect anything more. That said, if whoever made this point about men being forgetful is with a guy who really doesn't remember things they've planned or even her birthday, then maybe his actions are telling her something about how he feels. After all, actions speak louder than words.

7. They get all our friends' children's/partners' names wrong, even the ones we've just seen.

Some men are rubbish at remembering names. There's no way round that. Far more important is what your friends and their children and partners think of him and how he got on with them. If they like him and everyone got on well, why does it matter if he's not brilliant at remembering names? Would you rather he remembered every detail about everyone but wasn't liked so much? Of course not. Stop looking at the glass as half empty. Focus on the positives about him.

8. They are reluctant to go to bed, always finding a distraction in TV or the internet or anything, really.

If this really bothers you, try giving him a reason to go to bed. You know what I mean.

9. They 'suffer' from man flu and shameless hypochondria.

How do you know it's hypochondria? Come on, how do you really know? You don't. And how do you know if his 'man flu' is not the kind of horrible cold bordering on flu that would leave you in bed for a week? You don't. You can't know because you're not the one who's ill. So pipe down and be clever. Look after him when he's ill. If he's not really sick he'll get bored of it soon enough on his own. But don't tell him he's not ill and should be up and about doing things. That will annoy him and then he'll be ill *and* grumpy. Instead, humour him. Or just treat him how you would like to be treated when you're ill.

10. They spend our savings on ridiculous, expensive gadgets.

Yes, we like gadgets. We also like having the best, newest gadgets and we find them fascinating. I don't need to get into complicated male psychology to explain this. In a nutshell, gadgets are toys for adults and men like toys. End of explanation. Because we like them, sometimes we spend money on them. Occasionally too much money. But before you have a go at him, try comparing how much you spend on clothes in a year with how much he spends on gadgets. How much were those shoes? Half price in the sale, you say? How many pairs did you buy?

Three? Remember how many times a year sales happen and then go and do the maths on that.

11. They 'shower snork' — clearing their nose in the shower.

Do you ever see the evidence of this in the shower? I doubt it. Why? Because of the way a shower works – the water coming out of the shower takes everything down the plughole with it. So why does it matter if he snorks in the shower every now and then? It doesn't.

12. They leave bachelor-style coin pile-ups everywhere.

Unlike girls, we don't have purses to put coins in so we have to carry them in our pockets and very few things are as annoying as a pocket full of low-value coins. They are heavy, noisy, uncomfortable and probably won't even add up to enough to buy a coffee. So let's find a solution. Why not get him some kind of receptacle to put those annoying coins in? Make it quite big (a bottle or something similar) and then when it's full go to a bank (personally I like those coin weighing machines in Sainsbury's), get the money changed into notes and you'll get a very nice surprise. A couple of hundred pounds you didn't even know you had.

13. They have zero patience for shopping except when it's for themselves and then they are obsessed.

Not true. We don't mind shopping sometimes, as long as we feel like we are taking an active part, which means that our opinions actually mean something. But bear in mind that when it comes to choosing soft furnishings or your clothes, one cushion looks much like any other to us and if you are the one we love then to us you will look good in anything as long as it doesn't make you look like a whore or a librarian (somewhere in the middle is ideal). We also like shopping for TVs and things like that. Gadgets, basically. Let us get on with it. And remember who carries the heavy stuff on the way home.

14. They spend hours on the loo. Can it really be that time-consuming?

It's not time-consuming, it's relaxing. Sitting quietly and reading in a room where no one can disturb you is a very pleasant way to spend a few minutes. We like the peace and quiet. That's all. There's no great secret to it. And don't forget those few moments of solitude feel like a treat to us because men's loos are far more public than women's (I'm assuming you know what a urinal looks like). Remember that.

15. They send cryptic texts because they haven't given them enough thought.

There is a simple solution to the male communication issue. If there's something you want to know, ask questions that require simple answers, like 'yes' or 'no'. If a man isn't in the right mood or if he's being distracted by something like work, then it's likely he's not going to be very effective at making decisions or quickly giving you the information you want. He's concentrating on work so either ask simple questions or leave him alone. And if you don't get a yes or no answer, it's because he either doesn't care about the subject of the question or doesn't know what the answer is.

16. They always seem to want to break their necks skiing.

Until we have a serious accident doing something dangerous, we believe we're immortal, which is obviously dangerous too. And then, if we do have that serious accident and recover, we believe we can get over any injury, which is also dangerous. Yes, that's annoying and sometimes a bit stressful. But isn't it a good way to live? To keep trying things, enjoying yourself and accepting that sometimes you'll fall over and hurt yourself, but being determined to pick yourself up and carry on when you do get hurt? Yes, it is a very good way to live. So let men be men. I'm a good example – I hurt my knee badly in a skiing accident. Three years and four operations later I was skiing and playing rugby and squash again. Am I stupid? Probably. But at least I'm happy.

17. They drive like Formula One racers down the motorway because they believe they'll never get caught.

A driving ban or a couple of speeding fines teaches most of us a sharp lesson. If we don't learn that lesson then we deserve to be fined and banned. But make sure you let us learn for ourselves. If his driving scares you, tell him. If he doesn't listen, refuse to sit in the front seat until he starts making an effort. If that doesn't work, wear a blindfold. Just make sure he has a plausible explanation ready to give the police if they pull you over.

18. Their 'quick drink' disables their mobile phone and brings them back wasted at 4 a.m.

This is true. It happens frequently. The best way to deal with it is to accept that sometimes we are going to go out with our mates and get smashed. Unless it's happening too often (and too often means if it affects our work and home life) then you shouldn't worry. Once every week or two is fine. What you need to do is manage the situation. Accept that he'll be out late. Don't call him every five minutes. Tell him before he goes out that it's OK for him to tell you he's not sure when he'll be back and to go and enjoy himself. The night might only be a couple of pints, it might carry on until last orders or maybe you won't see him until 3 a.m. The thing is, men often don't know how long they're going to be out for. Our nights out take on lives of their own. Personally, if I'm out and having a good time with my friends, I don't want to have to look at my watch because I'm on a curfew, either self-imposed or otherwise. And you shouldn't worry about what he's doing. The vast, vast majority of guys will be talking rubbish with their mates, taking the mickey out of each other in the same way they have for years. Nothing sinister, just what men do. Let us be men.

19. They hate conflict and internalise things.

We don't prefer to let issues stew. We just aren't very good at talking about our feelings and so taking the ostrich approach – burying our head in the sand – is the easy option (we like easy options). If you don't want us to take this easy option, ask us gently what the matter is. Don't demand to be told, be gentle. Getting emotions out of some men is not easy. It requires patience and careful handling.

20. They burp and fart loudly and proudly.

True. But farting and burping are funny and if you can't see this, you're the one with the problem. Your sense of humour is far too mature. Get in touch with your inner child. You'll enjoy life far more. And do girls fart and burp? Yes, they do. Some are actually rather good at it (I'll mention no names).

21. They never make the bed because 'it needs to air'.

Of course beds need to air. Any man who says that is absolutely right. If you want him to make the bed more, don't hassle him about it. Just stop making it yourself and see what happens when he has to get into an unmade bed every evening. I suspect he'll start making more of an effort pretty quickly. This tactic was used successfully on me quite recently. It took a few weeks but she got there in the end and I'm now finally a committed bedmaker. At the age of thirty-three.

22. They won't let me choose what we watch on TV.

Quite right, too. Guys have better taste in TV programmes than girls and we like to watch what we like, particularly live sport. And please note that even with Sky+ we still like to watch sport as it's happening. That's what makes sport different to, say, *Desperate Housewives* or *Gossip Girl* (both of which I like, by the way) which can be recorded and watched later. If you're really, really annoyed about him not letting you choose what to watch, be clever.

Compromise. Use your feminine wiles and charms. Men can be wrapped around their girlfriend's little finger far more easily than you think. No, I'm not going to tell you how but I'll give you a clue: look back at number 2.

23. They worship their mother.

Of course we worship our mother. She brought us into the world and looked after us when we were too small to look after ourselves. And she will always love us, no matter what. Why shouldn't we worship her? What can possibly be wrong with that? Also, girls feel exactly the same about their own parents – and rightly so. In my experience very few girls really mind that their man is close to his mum and thinks highly of her. I happen to think that's healthy. I also think it's unhealthy for a girl to feel threatened by her boyfriend or husband's mother. And anyway, would you want to be with a guy who doesn't worship his mother? No, I didn't think so.

24. They lust after anything with bare legs and large breasts.

First, I don't like the phrase 'lust after'. It makes us sound like a bunch of animals who can't control their urges. We're not like that. But we do like looking at pretty girls. We're men, so of course we do. Especially in summer. I can't deny that. We can't help it. Honestly, we can't. It's as natural as being hungry or tired. But there are limits to how accepting you should be of this. If a guy is obviously staring at other girls while he's with you, then you shouldn't stand for it because that kind of behaviour is disrespectful. And if it upsets you, tell him. You're absolutely right to expect him to treat you better than that. At the same time, you're going to have to deal with the fact that all healthy men will look at people they find attractive. We can't help ourselves. But there's a middle ground between him being respectful and you accepting what men are. If this is causing a problem then you should work out where that middle ground is. Don't just bottle it up, tell him you don't like what he's doing.

25. They believe celebrities and models are 100% natural.

No we don't. The thing about men having crushes on famous girls is that we know what we're looking at is an illusion. We know these girls are airbrushed and we know that in real life models are normal girls who might well be bitchy or high maintenance or have many other unattractive qualities. We know that what we see on the pages of a magazine or on TV is an illusion. You don't need to be threatened by it because we're just enjoying the illusion. Here's a thing: I always think girls would be very surprised at how respectfully and fondly men talk about their wives or girlfriends when they're not around. Sure, we like looking at pictures of pretty girls. But do we love those girls? Would we like to build lives with those girls? Of course not.

The way a man feels about his girlfriend or wife is real. The way he feels about pretty girls in magazines is not.

Acknowledgements

To Carly Cook, Sam Eades, Jo Whitford and everyone else at Headline – thank you for taking my book on and for being so clever and enthusiastic.

Thank you to my brilliant agent Rowan Lawton at PFD. And to Lucy-Anne Holmes (writer of great books) for introducing me to her.

Jane Mulkerrins and Tracey Blake, my editors at the now sadly departed *London Lite*, thank you for starting all this by letting me write my column. It was great fun.

Thank you for too many things to mention to my mother Thea, sisters Rachel and Sarah and brother-in-law Dave.

Thank you to the following for their help at different stages of the book: Sarah Emsley; Andreas Campomar; Celia Walden; Chrissie Manby; Olly and Pip Saxby; Clare Conville; Magnus Boyd; Giles Vickers-Jones; Tim Andrews; Matt Potter; Martel Maxwell; Dominic Gill; Oli and Nicola; Dan and Claudine; Josh and Vanessa; Terence and Angela; Guy Dennis; Max and Mareike; Pally and Emily; Charlie and Sherradan; Ross, Lara, Noah and Kitty; Sean and Carla; Knighty and Vicky; Georgie and Nick; Matt

Nixson; Debbie; Jon and Sophie; Charlotte and Hamish; Nick and Astrid; and Lucy Abrahams.

Thank you to everyone who ever either told me a dating story, gave me some advice, asked what I thought about someone or who did anything at all which contributed in some way to this book. There are too many of you to name (and some of you wouldn't want to be named anyway) but I am very grateful to you all. And if I've upset or offended anyone along the way, I am truly sorry. I didn't mean to.

Finally, Charlotte, thank you for the last and best part of this story.